The principal difference between an adventurer and a suicide is that the adventurer leaves himself a margin of escape (the narrower the margin, the greater the adventure). A margin whose width and breadth may be determined by unknown factors, but whose successful navigation is determined by the measure of the adventurer's nerve and wits.

—Tom Robbins, *Even Cowgirls Get the Blues*

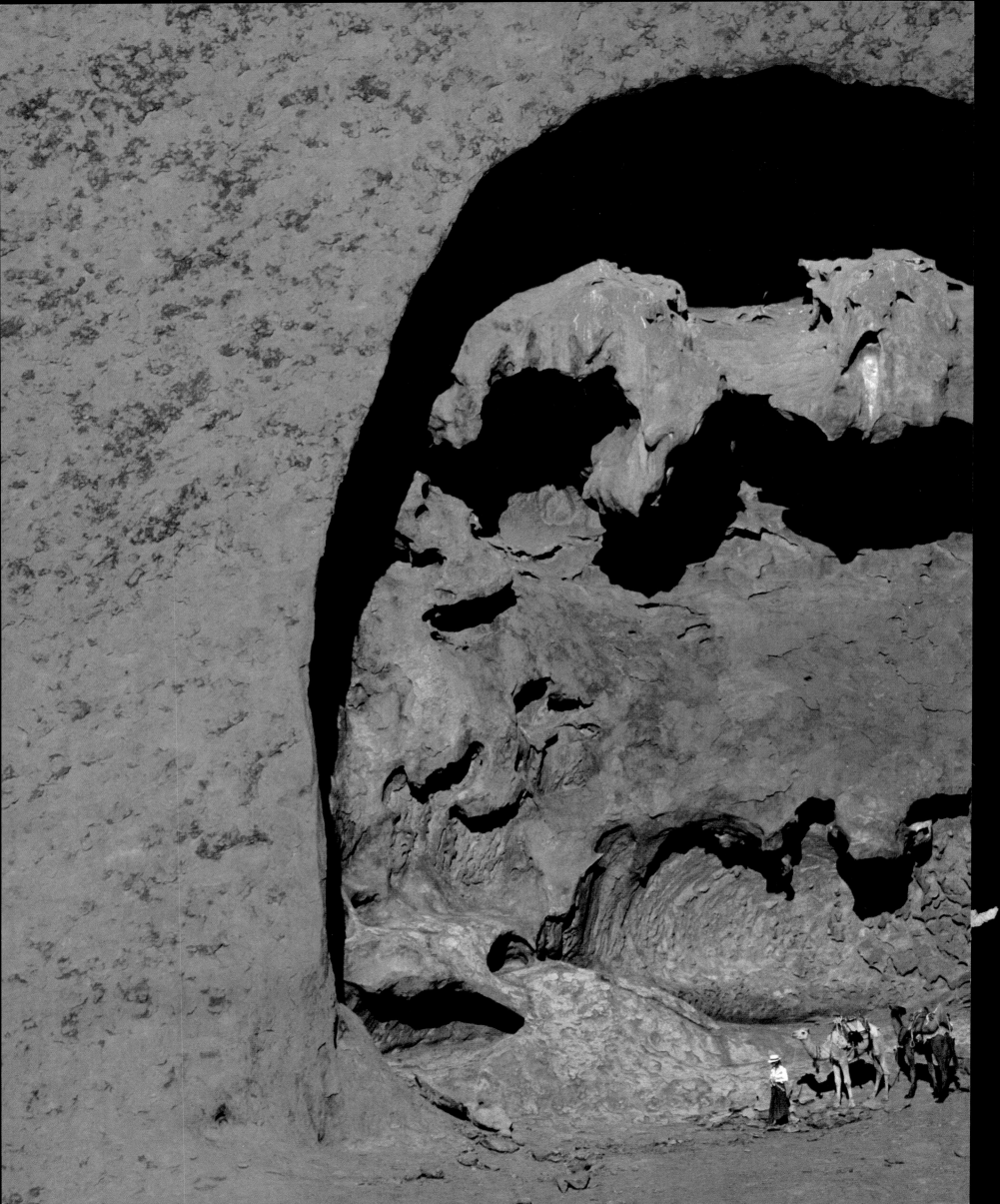

Robyn Davidson's journey was funded solely by the National Geographic Society.

The following companies generously provided the resources to make the publication of this book possible.

 Eastman Kodak Company

 Apple Computer, Inc.

From Alice to Ocean

Alone Across the Outback

Excerpted from Robyn Davidson's *Tracks*
Photographed by Rick Smolan

———

Designed by Thomas K. Walker
Edited by Rita D. Jacobs

▲
▼▼
Addison-Wesley Publishing Company

Reading, Massachusetts   Menlo Park, California   New York   Don Mills, Ontario
Wokingham, England   Amsterdam   Bonn   Sydney   Singapore   Tokyo   Madrid
San Juan   Paris   Seoul   Milan   Mexico City   Taipei

in association with
Against All Odds Productions

Library of Congress Cataloging-in-Publication Data

Davidson, Robyn. 1950–
          From Alice to Ocean : alone across the Outback / photographed by
Rick Smolan.
                    p.   cm.
          "Excerpted from Robyn Davidson's Tracks"
          ISBN 0-201-63216-0
          1. Australia--Description and travel--1981- 2. Davidson, Robyn,
1950- --Journeys--Australia. I. Smolan, Rick.   II. Davidson,
Robyn, 1950- Tracks. III. Title.
     DU105.D34 1992
     919.404'63--dc20   92-20886

Jacket and book design by Thomas K. Walker, GRAF/*x*
Jacket photographs by Rick Smolan

Printed in Japan
First printing, July 1992

10 9 8 7 6 5 4 3 2 1

PREFACE

*T*his book is deceptive. Although it may appear to be the adventure story of a young woman's 1700 mile trek alone across Australia's outback, in fact it's about a completely different kind of journey. *From Alice to Ocean* is the story of what happens when you discover that the most dangerous terrain is not the external but the internal.

This book is also the story of how I came to know a young woman whom I admired more than anyone I'd ever met. Unlike most people, whose instincts tell them to run when frightened, this woman's inner voice urged her to challenge and confront her fears head on. She was actually willing to risk her life for something she felt she had to do.

When I first met Robyn Davidson she was living in Alice Springs preparing to cross the outback alone. She didn't feel she owed the world an explanation, but she did need money to fund her trip. *National Geographic* was the perfect solution, an organization that would provide her with the resources she needed but not interfere with her plans. Or so she thought.

Robyn had never planned on sharing her trip, especially with a photojournalist. She certainly had never intended to write a book called *Tracks* about it or end up as one of Australia's leading authors. And for me, what began as a dream assignment that might lead to a *National Geographic* cover turned into a much more profound experience.

The one question people always ask is, "Why did Robyn make this trip?" It's the one question that even Robyn has never been able to answer. And as you read this book you'll discover that the "Why?" really doesn't matter. What does matter is that Robyn permitted herself to listen to the little voice inside herself that so many of us ignore.

As you turn these pages, remember Robyn's words, "You are as powerful and as strong as you allow yourself to be and the most difficult part of any endeavor is taking the first step." My deepest hope is that her journey will inspire you to look inside and find your own journey, your own "camel trip."

*I*ARRIVED IN THE ALICE AT FIVE A.M. WITH A DOG, SIX DOLLARS AND A SMALL SUIT-case full of inappropriate clothes. "Bring a cardigan for the evenings," the brochure said. A freezing wind whipped grit down the platform and I stood shivering, holding warm dog flesh, and wondering what foolishness had brought me to this eerie, empty train-station in the center of nowhere. I turned against the wind, and saw the line of mountains at the edge of town.

There are some moments in life that are like pivots around which your existence turns—small intuitive flashes, when you known you have done something correct for a change, when you think you are on the right track. I watched a pale dawn streak the cliffs with Day-glo and realized this was one of them. It was a moment of pure, uncomplicated confidence—and lasted about ten seconds.

Diggity wriggled out of my arms and looked at me, head cocked, piglet ears flying. I experienced that sinking feeling you get when you know you have conned yourself into doing something difficult and there's no going back. It's all very well, to set off on a train with no money telling yourself that you're really quite a brave and adventurous person, and you'll deal capably with things as they happen, but when you actually arrive at the other end with no one to meet and nowhere to go and nothing to sustain you but a lunatic idea that even you have no real faith in, it suddenly appears much more attractive to be at home on the kindly Queensland coast, discussing plans and sipping gins on the verandah with friends, and making unending lists of lists which get thrown away, and reading books about camels.

The lunatic idea was, basically, to get myself the requisite number of wild camels from the bush and train them to carry my gear, then walk into and about the central desert area. I knew that there were feral camels aplenty in the country. They had been imported in the 1850s along with their Afghani and North Indian owners, to open up the inaccessible areas, to transport food, and to help build the telegraph system and railways that would eventually cause their economic demise. When this happened, those Afghans had let their camels go, heart-broken, and tried to find other work. They were specialists and it wasn't easy. They didn't have much luck with government support either. Their camels, however, had found easy street—it was a perfect country for them and they grew and prospered, so that now there are approximately ten thousand roaming the free country and making a nuisance of themselves on cattle properties, getting

*Alice Springs, affectionately called
"the Alice" by its inhabitants, has
always been a magnet for artists
and desperados.*

shot at, and, according to some ecologists, endangering some plant species for which they have a particular fancy. Their only natural enemy is man, they are virtually free of disease, and Australian camels are now rated as some of the best in the world.

Several days later, I got a job at the pub. I could stay in the back room, the payment for which would be deducted from my first week's wages. Meals were provided. Perfect. That gave me time to suss out camel business.

Then I met Kurt, one of the camel men in town, who greeted me with as much enthusiasm as his Germanic nature would allow. He was dressed in an immaculate white outfit, with an equally crisp white turban. But for his ice-blue eyes, he looked like a bearded wiry Moor. Standing near him was like being close to a fallen power line—all dangerous, crackling energy. He was dark brown, stringy, with hands calloused and outsized from work and he was certainly the most extraordinary individual I had ever laid eyes on. I had barely got out my name before he had begun to tell me exactly how life was to be for the next eight months, grinning, gap-toothed, all the while.

"Now you vill come to verk for me here for eight months und zen you vill buy vone off my camelts, und I vill teach you to train zem and you vill get two vild vones und dat vill be dat. I haf just de animal for you. He hass only vone eye but, ha, dat does not matter—he is stronk and reliable enough for you, ya."

Kurt proceeded to outline my duties. Shit seemed to be the major problem. I was to follow the animals around all day and pick up the offending stuff. I was also to catch the animals at four in the morning, unhobble them (to allow them to graze at night they were hobbled by straps and a foot of chain around their front legs to prevent them going too far, too fast) and lead them home in a long line, nose to tail, ready for saddling. Two or three would be used for the day's work, leading tourists around the oval for a dollar a go, while the rest would be kept in the yards.

But Kurt treated me so badly that in a short period of time I burst. I lashed out at him, calling him every name under the sun and screaming that he had a snowflake's chance in hell of ever getting me to do his dirty work again. I'd die first. He was stupefied and knew he had sized me up wrongly. But he was too proud to apologize and the next morning I moved back to the pub.

*G*ETTING CAMELS OR EVEN INFORMATION WAS TURNING OUT TO be infinitely harder than I had thought. Word of my scheme had spread and it brought much derisive laughter and enough useless and incorrect information to stock a library of the absurd. Suddenly everyone, it seemed, knew all there was to know about camels.

One does not have to delve too deeply to discover why some of the world's angriest feminists breathed crisp blue Australian air during their formative years, before packing their kangaroo-skin bags and scurrying over to London or New York or any place where the antipodean machismo would fade gently from their battle-scarred consciousnesses like some grisly nightmare at dawn. Anyone who has worked in a men-only bar in Alice Springs will know what I mean.

To really come to grips with the Australian cult of misogyny, one has to plod back through all two hundred years of white Australia's history, and land on the shore of the "wide brown land" with a bunch of hard-done-by whingeing convicts. Actually, the place where they landed was relatively green and inviting, the wide brown stuff was to come later. One imagines life was none too easy in the colony, but the boys learnt to stick together and when they'd done their stretch, if they were still sound of limb, they ventured into the forbidding country beyond to try to scratch a pitiful living. They were tough and they had absolutely nothing to lose. And they had alcohol to soften the blow. By the 1840s it began to dawn on the residents

At first Robyn was determined to be alone and to focus only on her trip. But slowly Jenny Green (above) and her friend Toly Sawenko, two other idealistic travellers who were indignant about the Australian Government's treatment of Aborigines, became her closest mates.

that something was missing—sheep and women. The former they imported from Spain, a stroke of genius that was to set Australia on the economic map; the latter they brought over in boats from the poorhouses and orphanages of England. Since there were never enough to go round (women, that is) one can visualize only too clearly the frenzied rush on the Sydney wharves when the girls came bravely sailing in. Such a traumatic racial memory is hard to blot out in a mere century, and the cult is sustained and revitalized in every pub in the country, especially in the outback where the stereotyped image of the Aussie male is still so sentimentally clung to. The modern day manifestation is almost totally devoid of charm. He is biased, bigoted, boring and, above all, brutal. His enjoyments in life are limited to fighting, shooting and drinking. To him a mate includes anyone who is not a wop, wog, pom, coon, boong, nigger, rice-eye, kyke, chink, Iti, nip, frog, kraut, commie, poofter, slope, wanker, and yes, sheila, chick or bird.

One night in the pub one of the kinder regulars whispered to me, "You ought to be more careful, girl, you know you've been nominated by some of these blokes as the next town rape case. You shouldn't be so friendly."

I was devastated. What had I done but patted the odd shoulder or helped out the occasional paralytic or listened in silence to some heart-breaking hard luck story. I felt really frightened for the first time.

During those first months I was often overwhelmed by such despair that I thought of packing up and going home, beaten. This was countered effectively by a singularly cunning manoeuvre on the part of Kurt, who had overcome his fierce pride and talked me into going back to work for him. After complimenting me on my work, he informed me of a new financial arrangement he had thought up. He would keep me working there for the eight months, then for two or three he would help me build my saddles and gear and prepare for the trip, after which he would give me three camels of my choice, free, to be returned when the trip was finished. It was, of course, too good to be true. I knew that he was playing with me, knew it, and then rejected the knowledge because I needed to believe. I looked into his eyes, through which self-interest shone like a torch, and accepted. It was a gentleman's agreement. Kurt refused to sign anything, saying that was not the way he did business, but as everyone knew, me included, Kurt

Robyn had rescued her Kelpie "Diggity" as a puppy from certain death in a medical research laboratory. Diggity returned the favor in Alice Springs by alerting her against human intruders and the poisonous snakes that often slithered through her room at Basso's farm.

had never been a gentleman. He had me over a barrel but there was nowhere else to go if I wanted to breathe life into my dream.

My social life in Alice centered around Basso's Farm, a dilapidated old stone house occupied by the potters and leather craftsmen who had become my friends. They were archetypal hippies with attractive desperado overtones, who were friendly, hospitable and talked to me in a language I had almost forgotten. I would wedge in an hour or two at Basso's most nights, sitting and drinking with friends, belly-aching about Kurt, and meeting small rare handfuls of sympathetic, friendly Alice-Springians. But by this stage I had become emotionally remote from outsiders. I was withdrawn and found it hard to relax, especially when I had to face being introduced as someone with a label—something that always instigates an identity crisis. "I'd like you to meet Robyn Davidson, she's taking camels across Australia." I didn't know quite how to deal with that one except to fall in with it. Another trap. It was the inauspicious beginning of the "camel lady" image which I should have nipped in the bud right there.

I WORKED FOR KURT MONTHS LONGER THAN I SHOULD HAVE. IT FINALLY BECAME clear that he would never honor his promises. So I left and went to work for Sallay Mahomet who was to become a friend, camel-guru and saviour. He told me that anyone who could put up with Kurt for that long deserved a break, and he promptly produced a signed guarantee that if I came to work for him for a couple of months he would give me two of his wild camels.

The most important things Sallay taught me were how to use ropes to tie up a camel, how to carve and whittle nose-pegs from white-wood or mulga, how to splice, how to fix saddles, in fact all the myriad little bits of knowledge that would play such an important part in my survival out bush. He was an endless mine of such information. He had been with camels all his life, and although his relationship to them was anything but sentimental, and although he treated them somewhat roughly for my soft-hearted tastes, he was the best camel-man in town. He knew the animals as well as the back of his own hand, and some of that knowledge seeped into me and came out when I least expected it on my journey.

I had been in Alice for almost a year now and I was a changed woman. It seemed that I had always been there, that anything I may have been before was a dream belonging to someone else. My grip on reality was a little shaky. I wanted to see my friends again because I was beginning to realize how removed from everything but camels and madmen I had become.

I had made a choice instinctively, and only later had given it meaning. The trip had never been billed in my mind as an adventure in the sense of something to be proved. And it struck me then that the most difficult thing had been the decision to act, the rest had been merely tenacity—and the fears were paper tigers. One really could do anything one had decided to do whether it were changing a job, moving to a new place, divorcing a husband or whatever, one really could act to change and control one's life; and the procedure, the process, was its own reward.

Because camels are cud chewers, bits can't be used to control them, so a noseline must be used to steer or lead them instead. A wooden peg, (below) carved and whittled out of white-wood or mulga, is implanted in the nostril (right) and a string is attached to it. Hobbles and lengths of chain (bottom) are used to keep the camels from wandering too far and too quickly.

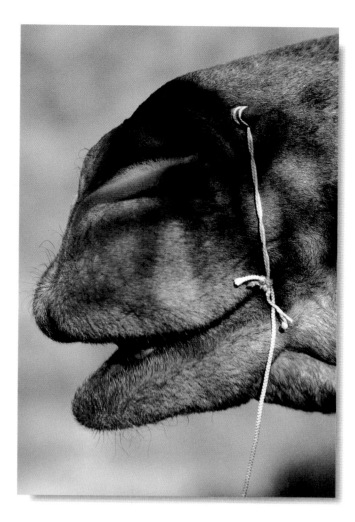

*I*HAD TO BEGIN TRAINING MY FIRST CAMEL, ZELEIKA, FOR RIDING AND CARRYING a pack. This was not easy—I had no money to buy equipment, no saddle to put on her back so that it wouldn't fall off every time she bucked, and I had lost most of my nerve. So I rode her bareback, quietly, up and down the soft sand of the creek, not asking her to do too much—just trying to win her confidence and keep her quiet and protect my own skin. She was in such poor condition that I constantly had to balance the need for training against not allowing her to worry herself back into a skeleton. Camels always lose weight during training. Instead of eating, they spend all day thinking about what you are going to do to them. Zeleika also had a lovely gentle nature which I did not want to spoil. I could walk up to her anywhere in the wild, whether she was hobbled or not, and catch her, even though I could feel her muscles tighten into hard lumps with tension and fear. Her only dangerous fault was her willingness to kick. Now, a camel can kick you in any direction, within a radius of six feet. They can strike with their front legs, and kick forward, sideways or backwards with the back. One of those kicks could snap you in half like a dry twig. Teaching her to accept hobbles and side-lines was not an easy business. In fact, it was ulcer-inducing if not death-producing and required infinite patience and bravery, neither of which I was particularly blessed with but I had no choice. To quieten her I had to tie her to a tree on the halter and encourage her to eat rich and expensive hand-feed, while I groomed her all over, picked up her legs, played loud music on a tape recorder and got her used to having things around her feet and on her back, all the time talking talking talking. When she did let fly with one of those terrible legs, it was out with the whip. She soon learnt that this kicking got her nowhere and that it was easier to be nice, even if that niceness didn't come from the heart.

Because camels' necks are so strong, the nose-line is essential for a riding animal. It is almost impossible to control them with just a halter, unless you have super-human strength. They cannot take a bit like a horse as they are cud-chewers. The only alternative is a jaw-line, which I sometimes used in training before the peg wound healed, but which cut into their soft bottom lip. So the nose-peg method is best. They are usually given only one of these, which sticks out the side of either nostril. To it is attached a piece of string, strong enough to cause pain when it is jerked, but not so strong that it will not snap long before the peg is pulled through the flesh. This string is attached to the outside of the peg, then split under the jaw and used simply as reins. Once the peg wound has healed, this method causes no more discomfort than a bit does to a horse.

Zeleika, Robyn's first camel, had been caught in the wild and tamed, as well as a wild camel could be. Zelly never lost her "desert smarts" and instinctively knew which plants were safe to eat and which were deadly. Because she had been wild, she took being hobbled as an insult and in the beginning often asserted her independence by kicking.

26

Sallay came out to visit me one day to see how I was doing. I took him down to Zelly and he looked her over, commenting on how well she looked and how quiet she was. He then stood back for a minute, rubbed his chin thoughtfully, and shot me a sideways glance.

"You know what I think, girl?"

"What do you think, Sallay?"

He rubbed those expert hands over her belly again. "I think you've got yourself a pregnant camel."

"What? Pregnant?" I yelled. "But that's fantastic. No wait, that's not fantastic. What if she has it on the trip?"

Sallay laughed and patted me on the shoulder. "Believe me, having a baby camel on your trip would be the least of your worries. When it's born you just tie it up in a sack, hoist it on its mother's back, and within a few days it will trot along behind with the best of them. In fact, it would be a good thing for you, because you can tie the baby up at night and be sure that the mother won't go too far. Could solve one of your main problems, eh? Well, I hope she is, for your sake. Should be a nice little calf, too, if that wild black bull I saw her running with was the father."

As Robyn's band of camels grew so did her affection for them. Under her growing expertise they began to develop distinct personalities. "They are the most intelligent creatures I know except for dogs and I would give them an I.Q. rating roughly equivalent to eight-year-old children."

*W*HEN IT FINALLY CAME, MY STROKE OF GOOD FORTUNE WAS A LITTLE UPWARD spiral of fate that made up for all the downers put together. Kurt had disappeared overnight, in a puff of dust, like a genie, and had sold the place secretly to some station people. Although I had not been working for Kurt for several months, he told the buyers I went along with the ranch and would teach them all they needed to know about camels. They knew precisely nothing. I went to see them. "Look," I explained, "I do not go along with the place, but if you are willing to give me the two camels I want, I will certainly teach you all I know."

And then Dookie, that most gentle of Kurt's beasts, took a turn and frightened the socks, shirt, shoes and trousers off the new owner. Luckily I was there.

Dookie had transmogrified. Dookie was coming for me with a decidedly Kurtish look in his eyes which were rolling back into his head like spun marbles. Dookie was making burbling noises and white froth was blowing out the side of his mouth. Dookie was completely berserk. For the first time in his young life he was taken over by those uncontrollable urges of a bull in season. He began thrashing his head and neck around like a whip. He was trying to gallop at me in his hobbles. He was going to try to knock me down and sit on me and crush the life and blood out of my body.

"Dookie?" I said, backing off. "Hey, Dook, this is me," I gasped as I made a bee-line for the gate. I hopped all five feet of it like Popeye after spinach. Dookie was oblivious to the new owner who stood frozen, cowering against the wall of rocks, on the wrong side of the fence. It was me Dookie wanted.

"Get out of there," I screamed as Dookie tried to bite off my head at the neck. "For Christ's sake, man, get me the whip, get me the hobble chain, get me the cattle prodder," I yelled maniacally as Dookie pinned me to my side of the gate with his twisted neck and tried to squash me into a cardboard replica. He was leaning into the fence now, trying to smash it so he could get at me. I could not believe this. This was some nightmare from which I would wake screaming at any moment. My Dookie was a Jekyll and Hyde, a killer, a mad mad mad bull. The man was galvanized into action. He brought out all those instruments of torture. A cattle prod throws a huge number of volts and this I pressed into Dookie's snapping lips while I beat him as hard as I could across the back of the head with the hobble chain. I could barely hear my own whimpering through the fracas. Dookie did not feel a thing. He was like a windmill with teeth. I got away from the gate for a second and my mind crystallized. I raced for some ropes, a wood plank, and an iron bar weighing fifteen pounds. About five feet from the

Like the other camel men in Alice, Sallay Mahomet, an Australian-born Afghan camel handler, was initially dubious about Robyn's ability to carry out her plan. Sallay, whose business was exporting wild Australian camels back to Arabia (!), eventually agreed to trade Robyn two camels in return for a few months work.

other side of the fence, Dookie's side, was a gum tree. I walked up my side of the fence till I was in line with it. Dookie followed me bellowing and snorting and thrashing. I bent down to his front legs, threw the rope through the hobbles, cleared the fence, and quickly, oh so quickly, brought the rope around the tree and heaved with all my might. I had him tied to the tree by the legs now and I only hoped that all of it would hold. I then proceeded to bash that creature over the back of the neck with the wood, until it snapped, and then with the iron bar. Down he would go, half conscious, then up again to attack. I had the super-human strength you only get when you are in a flat, adrenalin-pumping panic, and fighting for your life. Suddenly, Dookie sat down with a thump, shook his head a few times, and remained sitting quietly grinding his teeth.

I waited a moment, bar poised in mid-air. "Are you all right, Dookie?" I whispered. No reaction. "Dookie, I'm going to put this nose-line on you now and if you go crazy again, I swear I'll kill you." Dookie looked at me through his long graceful lashes. Butter wouldn't melt in his mouth.

I returned to the man. "Well, ha ha, that's bulls for you," I said, trying to will a little colour back into my cheeks. I was drenched in sweat and shaking like a leaf in a high wind. His mouth was still open, gawping.

"Do ah, do bulls often act like that?" he said.

"Oh hell yeeees," I answered, beginning to see the light at the end of the tunnel. "Christ, bulls attack like that all the time." I had him now. I was almost overcome with glee. I tried to slather a look of sisterly concern over my face. "Yeah, you want to keep your kids away from those bulls, that's for sure."

By nine o'clock I was running down the creek towards home, whooping and shouting, leaping and laughing hysterically. He had sold me the two bulls for seven hundred dollars—money I didn't have but which I could borrow. They weren't the two I would have chosen, but I was in no position to look a gift-camel in the mouth. Dookie, king of kings, and Bub that incorrigible little joker were mine. I had my three camels.

Bub, Robyn's third camel, was a natural clown, a creature driven in one direction by unbridled curiosity and in the other by a cowardly fear of his own shadow. Of Robyn's camels, Bub was the most easily spooked.

ONE CONTINUES TO LEARN THINGS IN LIFE, THEN PROMPTLY FORGET THEM. AND I should have known by now that pride always comes before a fall. I was beginning to feel cocky. I had my three camels, Zeleika, Dookie and Bub. I was beginning to feel that I was in control of events, self-congratulatory, complacent. Life was good and bountiful. Nothing else could go wrong, statistics were against it. I had had my various runs of bad luck. My friends were around me. I was in no danger. Toly was spending most of his weekends with us, and we all adored him. He worked as a teacher at Utopia, an Aboriginal-owned cattle station, 150 miles north. And if he whisked my good friend Jen away for days at a time, and if I could never go with them because I was chained to the camels, I tried hard not to be envious. They left big empty spaces when they disappeared.

One of the little things that cropped up was that I would spend a whole day tracking my camels. Their footprints would become all mixed up and it was difficult to sort today's from yesterday's. There were six or seven directions in which they would head out to feed, most of these being rocky places where tracking was not easy. They would secrete themselves away in hidden valleys or dense thickets where I could not see them—they blended in so well with the khaki and reds of the landscape. They had bells on, but I swear they held their necks perfectly still and stiff when they smelt me on the wind. When they saw me, of course, it was all, "Hail fellow, well met. Clang clang." And, "What kept you so long?" And, "How nice to see you, Rob, what titbits have you got in your pockets?" It got to the point where, instead of catching them, I could simply unhobble them and watch them gallop and buck all the way home, or else crawl up behind some hump and get a lift. Dookie had lost all his bull-headed silliness with the hot weather, and the three were now an inseparable team. Zelly was plumping out in all the right places and her udder was swelling nicely. They had well-defined relationships to one another. Zeleika was the street-smart, crafty, unfazable, self-possessed leader. She was wiser than the other two put together in the ways of the wild. She was the Prime Minister, while Dookie was nominally king, but if anything untoward happened he was the first to hide behind her skirts. And Bub was in love with Dookie. Dookie was his hero, and he was quite brave as long as he had Dookie's rear end in front of his nose. He totally lacked any desire or capacity to lead. If Dookie was Hardy, then Bub was definitely his Laurel.

It was on one of these mornings, after I had tracked them down the creek, that something happened which made me believe the world had stopped. Bub

As the time for her departure neared, Robyn's friends were concerned that she was beginning to identify too closely with her camels.

was lying on his side. I thought he was sunbathing so I sat next to his head and said, "Arra (get going), you lazy little sod, it's time to go home," and put a lolly in his mouth. (They liked jelly-beans and long sticks of licorice best.) Instead of leaping up to see what other goodies I had, he continued to lie there, chewing the sweet half-heartedly, and I knew something was dreadfully wrong. I got him up and saw that he was standing on three legs. I lifted the foot and checked the soft pad underneath—there was a gash, with a wedge of glass stuck in it. Kurt had had to shoot one of his animals because of just such a wound. These pads were meant for soft sand, not sharp objects, and were the most vulnerable part of the animals. Inside the pad is a squishy, elastic sort of bladder; when pressure is put on the foot, any hole will therefore widen. It is impossible to keep them off a leg, because they need that pressure for circulation. The cut had gone straight through the bottom of the foot, and up through the hairy top surface. I thought he was finished. I sat there and wept on that river-bank for a good half hour. I howled and howled. Camels are such hardy animals, I thought, it's just sheer perverse and cruel fate that has caused this to happen. Who is it up there who hates me? I shook my fist and howled some more. Diggity licked my face and Zelly and Dook bent down to offer their condolences. I had Bub's big ugly head in my lap. He continued to eat jelly-beans, lapping up the attention and playing Camille admirably. I pulled myself together, took the glass out of the foot as carefully as possible, and led him slowly home. The vets I knew were out of town, I discovered when I pedalled in to the clinic, and a new inexperienced boy was doing the locum for them. He came out to Basso's to look at Bubby, stood six feet away from the camel, said, "Hmm, he's got a cut in his foot all right." And gave me some injections for tetanus. Not much help. I had met two women at the restaurant, Kippy and Cherie,

Peter Latz, an ethnobotanist, (above left) helped plan the 1700 mile route across the Gibson Desert. Peter's extraordinary knowledge of desert plant-foods became a vital tool in Robyn's outback survival kit.

who were terminal animal lovers and who managed a veterinary practice in Perth. I pedalled in to work that night and told them what had happened. They came out the next day, their last in town, lanced the top hole so that it would drain, and prescribed hot water and Condy's crystals. The foot was to be immersed in a bucket of the stuff and I was to massage the wound, cleaning it out thoroughly. Wonderful women, they gave me hope again.

Toly and Jenny then built me a large holding yard out the back of Basso's, with old star pickets, scraps of wire and netting, and various other assortments of stuff which we picked up here and there. It was an excellent yard. I kept Bubby in there, treated his foot three times a day and prayed. This went on for a few weeks, and I could never be sure if the foot was healing or if rotten flesh was growing in there like mushrooms. Bub did not enjoy the treatments and neither did I. "Keep that bloody foot still, you little mongrel, or I'll chop it off at the knee." He gradually came round. Soon the foot looked healthy enough for me to let him go with the others, who had been hanging around the house like bad smells, putting their long necks into the kitchen, or standing expectantly, eyes greedily bulging every time we sat in the garden for a cup of tea. My friends were falling in love with them as much as I was, though they wrongly accused me of projecting human attributes on to them. We laughed at them for hours. They were better to watch than a Marx Brothers movie.

And then one bright sunny day it happened. They disappeared. Into the wild blue yonder, just like that, poof. No camels, no adorable do-no-wrong beasties. They had deserted me, the ungrateful, cunning, fickle, deceitful two-timing traitors—pissed off. Headed for the hills as fast as their hobbled legs could carry them. It was quite usual for them to wander short distances but this time it was serious. Maybe they were bored, and looking for adventure. But I suspected that Zeleika was the culprit. She was going home thank you very much, leading the others back to her herd where there were no such things as saddles and work. She was not as easily conned and bribed with hand-outs and cuddles as the others. Not as spoilt. And she had not for a minute forgotten the sweetness of freedom.

I headed out as usual that morning with Dig to find their tracks. It took me about an hour to pick them up—they were heading almost due east, out into

As the two years of preparation drew to a close, Robyn was able to sit back and enjoy her camels' antics. These were going to be her companions for the next six months. They were spirited and she knew she had chosen well. "I loved them all with an anthropomorphizing devotion. No matter how much I discovered about them, there was always more to learn."

the wild hills. I followed for a couple of miles, thinking that they would be just around the next corner and imagining I could hear bells tinkling not too far away. There is a little wedge-bill bird in that country that sounds just like a camel-bell, and it often had me fooled. It was getting very hot, so I took off my shirt, put it under a bush and told Dig to wait there for me until I got back, which I thought would be half an hour at most. I was now into rough uninhabited country—there was no one and nothing for countless miles. I was vaguely wondering what on earth could have induced the camels to wander this far, this fast. But I wasn't worried. I was hot on their trail—their droppings were still moist. I could see from the tracks that one of them had broken a leather strap and was dragging a chain. And I walked. And I walked. And I walked. I crossed the Todd River and immersed my boiling body in a cool pool and drank as much as I could. I wet my trousers and wound them around my head and still I walked. My speed slowed down now as I was in stonier country. And all the while I was thinking, "What's happening here? Has someone chased them? What's going on, for Christ's sake?" I walked thirty miles that day, tantalized by the belief that they were just a minute ahead of me, but I heard nothing but phantom bells dinging inside my own skull, and saw nary a camel. I returned late at night to find poor Diggity almost fretted away, still sitting under the bush, her pink tongue dry as a bone, and a groove of worried dog-prints a hundred yards in the home direction, and a hundred yards in my direction. But she had stayed, faithful creature, despite what must have been an unbearable anxiety and an equally unbearable thirst. She was so relieved to see me, she almost turned herself inside out.

The next day I left better prepared. I reached yesterday's point fairly quickly—it was only about eight miles as the crow flies—to find that the tracks petered out a mile or two later into rocky escarpments. I went home and rang up all the station owners out in that direction. No, they had not seen any camels, they usually shot them anyway. But they would keep a look-out for mine.

Then I found some generous people in town with a light aircraft who offered to take me up into the clouds to look for them. I knew vaguely where they would be, I thought, then realized that if they could go that far in one day, they could go seven times as far, in any direction, in the week that had passed. I felt

Just when Robyn began to trust the camels she woke up one morning and they had disappeared. She and Diggity tried to track them into the outback by foot with no luck.

despondent. We flew in a grid pattern, much lower than regulations ordained, for about an hour. Not a sign.

"They they are," I screamed, strangling the co-pilot from behind.

"No, donkeys."

"Oh."

And as I sat, straining my eyes out the window of the plane something rose to the surface which had been buried since the moment I decided on this trip, more than two years before. I didn't have to go through with it. Losing the camels was the perfect excuse. I could pack my bags and say, "Oh, well, I did my best," and go on home, free of this obsession, this compulsion. I had never really considered doing it of course. I had conned myself into believing I would but no one would be crazy enough to do such a thing. It was dangerous. Now, even my camels would be happy, and that would be that.

And I recognized then the process by which I had always attempted difficult things. I had simply not allowed myself to think of the consequences, but had closed my eyes, jumped in, and before I knew where I was, it was impossible to renege. I was basically a dreadful coward, I knew that about myself. The only possible way I could overcome this was to trick myself with that other self, who lived in dream and fantasy and who was annoyingly lackadaisical and unpractical. All passion, no sense, no order, no instinct for self-preservation. The excruciating thing was that those two selves were now warring with each other. I wanted desperately to find those camels, and I wanted desperately not to find them.

The pilot snapped me back to the present dilemma.

"Well, what do you want to do? Shall we call it a day?"

I would have said yes, but my friend Julie talked us into one more run.

And on that final turn, there they were. Julie spotted them, we took a position and flew back to the runway. And that was the point at which all my disparate selves agreed to do the trip.

N OW THAT THE TRIP WAS REAL, NOW THAT I KNEW IT WAS ACTUALLY GOING TO happen, I was horrified by the amount of work I had to do to prepare. And I was at a complete loss as to how I could lay my hands on the money to buy equipment and so on. The camels took up so much of my time that it was impossible to get more work in town. I could borrow money from family or friends, but I decided against that. I had always been poor, always lived on a shoe-string, and if I did borrow the money it could take me years to pay it back. Besides, I hated being in debt, and it seemed unfair to ask my family to donate money to a project which, I knew, already had them worried half into the grave. And most of all, I wanted to do the thing on my own without outside interference or help. An attempt at a pure gesture of independence.

While I was sitting at Basso's, fretting, worrying and chewing my nails up to the elbow, a young man, a photographer, arrived with a friend of mine. He took a few photos of us and of the camels but, for an event which had such far-reaching effects, the meeting was inauspicious to the point where I had forgotten about it the next day.

But Rick came again, this time for dinner with a group of people from town. And once more, I was so preoccupied that only a few things stand out in my memory. He was a nice enough boy— rather Jimmy Olsenish I thought— one of those amoral immature photojournalists who hop from trouble spot to trouble spot on the globe without ever having time to see where they are or be affected by it. He had the most beautiful hands I had ever seen on anybody—long tapering fingers that wrapped around his cameras like frog's feet; and I remember vaguely some tepid arguments concerning the morality of and justification for taking clichéd photographs of Aborigines in the creek-bed for Time magazine when you knew precisely nothing about them, and didn't much want to. And, oh yes, I remember he stared at me a lot, as if I were a little bit touched. Just those few things, nothing more remains.

He also talked me into writing to *National Geographic* for sponsorship. I had tried this years before, only to receive a polite refusal. But when they left that night, I wrote what I drunkenly considered a brilliant letter, and thought no more about it.

So far, people had said that I wanted to commit suicide, that I wanted to do penance for my mother's death, that I wanted to prove a woman could cross a desert, that I wanted publicity. Some begged me to let them come with me; some were threatened, jealous or inspired; some thought it was a joke. The trip was

Robyn's final few days in Alice would be the last time for a long while that she would be able to relax with a friend in a restaurant or play with a tamed kangaroo. She found herself treasuring the little things she had always taken for granted.

beginning to lose its simplicity.

Why was everyone so goddamn affected by this trip, adversely or otherwise? Had I stayed back home, studying half-heartedly or working in gambling clubs or drinking at the Royal Exchange Pub and talking about politics—that would have been quite acceptable. I would not have been up for all these astounding projections.

Weeks later I received a cable saying, "Of course we are most interested..." from *National Geographic.* Now, all this time I had known, or rather, one of me had known, that they would accept my proposal. How could they not? I had written such a cajoling, confident letter. Of course I must take the money and run. I had no choice. I needed hand-made water canteens, a new saddle, three pairs of stalwart sandals, not to mention food and pocket money. I also knew at some level that it meant the end of the trip as I had conceived it: knew that it was the wrong thing to do—a sell-out. A stupid but unavoidable mistake. It meant that an international magazine would be interfering—no, not overtly, but would have a vested interest in, would therefore be a subtle, controlling factor in, what had begun as a personal and private gesture. And it meant that Rick would have to be around occasionally to take pictures—something I put out of my mind immediately, saying that he would only come for a day or two at a time, and then only three times during the trip. I would hardly notice his presence. But I knew that this would alter irrevocably the whole texture of what I wanted to do, which was to be alone, to test, to push, to unclog my brain of all its extraneous debris, not to be protected, to be stripped of the all the social crutches, not to be hampered by any outside interference whatsoever, well meant or not. But the decisions had already been made. Practicality had won the day. I had sold a great swatch of my freedom and most of the trip's integrity for four thousand dollars. That's the breaks.

But first I had to meet the people from *Geographic* in Sydney. The night before I was to wing my way south, we all gathered in the caravan with the object

Robyn would never directly answer questions about what was compelling her to undertake this risky journey. Each of her friends had a different theory and many of them wanted to join her. But Robyn was adamant—she was going to do the trip alone. (Above and left, Robyn and Diggity swimming in Redbank Gorge).

of fitting me out for the journey. Julia, a friend of Jenny's, was there too, and I played dressing-up with their clothes. All I had were old baggy men's bowling trousers, ten-year-old bright red patent-leather dancing pumps, shirts you could spit through, sarongs with holes in the wrong places, derelict running shoes, and a couple of dresses stained with all manner of camel excreta. We agreed that arriving at a posh hotel for a conference with the heads of *National Geographic* dressed like that would be a bit too authentic. They might decide I was a bad risk, too much of a loony tune. So I tizzed myself up in tight jeans and whip-chic high-heeled suicide boots. It did nothing for my confidence. I gathered my maps together and tucked them impressively and efficiently under my arm, so as to appear capable and sure of what I was doing, then realized that I didn't know very much about the country I was about to go over, should they ask me any embarrassing questions. I decided to fake it.

I suffered during that dress rehearsal. My friends clapped hands to foreheads and groaned theatrically. I hadn't even planned out the route coherently yet. And I suffered. I suffered that sickening, palm-sweating, pre-exam terror all the way to Sydney and right through the two hours with Rick, right up to the moment when I walked into the bar to meet these extraordinary Americans who were going to give me money for nothing—and then I switched into cool, suave little-miss-has-it-all-together-and-you-might-be-lucky-enough-to-get-some. The interview took fifteen minutes and then everyone agreed that it was a fascinating idea and I obviously knew a great deal about the country and yes, *Geographic* would send me the cheque very soon and how charming to meet you my dear, we look forward to seeing you in Washington when you come to write the story and what a marvellous book it would make have you thought of writing a book dear and good luck goodbye.

"Rick, do you mean to tell me they've actually said yes?"

"Yes, they've said yes."

"Rick, do you mean to tell me it's that easy?"

(Laughing) "You were great. Really. You didn't look scared at all."

My hysterical cackle kept up for about two hours. I was on an untouchable high. I had sprouted metaphorical wings. The trip was real. The last hurdle has been cleared with flying colours. I hooted and clapped Rick on the back. I drank margaritas and tipped waiters. I beamed at elevator men. I surprised hotel

The lineup: Baby Goliath, his mother Zelly, Bub, a gelded male, and big Dookie, an older gelding.

Robyn Davidson,
c/o The Post Office,
Alice Springs, N.T. 5750
Australia

Joe Judge (Senior Assistant Editor)   31st December, 1976
National Geographic Magazine,
17th & M Streets, N.W.,
Washington D.C.,
U.S.A. 20036

Dear Sir,

I wrote to you almost a year ago now in the hope that you would consider publishing a story on my proposed camel trip across Western Australia. You weren't interested at the time, but since then I have gone through two years preparation and when I discussed it with David Lewis he seemed to think you may yet be.

I have my three camels (and one small calf) trained and ready to go and have been working with them solidly for the past eighteen months. They are perfectly reliable beasts. Most of the equipment is already bought and I have done a few test runs into the semi-desert surrounding Alice Springs.

Living with the Aborigines has taught me a lot about survival — tracking, bush, food gathering etc. I would like to be able to take Aboriginal guides with me occasionally along the route to learn something of their methods of navigation.

The general plan at present, is to leave Alice Springs in late April and take a leisurely ride to Ayers Rock via some of the more beautiful gorges along the McDonnell Ranges and Finke River. From the Rock I shall push on to Docker River and Giles Meteorological Station just west of the border, following the track known as the "Gunbarrel Highway". The real Western Desert then has to be crossed and I shall probably take the track to Wilune. The dangerous leg of the journey then being over, I shall decide whether to go straight to the West coast or down to Perth.

The trip will take me through some of the most beautiful and some of the most barren country the Western Desert can show. I will be travelling alone, save the dog and camels, and the trip should take six to eight months.

As I shall be following roads and four-wheel-drive tracks most of the way, there will be ample opportunities and facilities en route for filming, photographing, talking or whatever else National Geographic journalists have to do. I shall have a Nikkonos camera with me as well. I have some photos of me, my animals and the surrounding countryside, along with a map of the intended route, taken by a Time photographer, which I shall send you if you are interested.

I have written to you because I feel that National Geographic, a magazine of international repute, would be the most suitable to cover the story. I look forward to hearing from you in the near future.

Yours faithfully,

Robyn Davidson

maids with my cheery hellos. I swung down King's Cross like a million dollars. And then I slowly collapsed. Like a bicycle tyre with a slow leak.

What had I done?

Rick was flabbergasted at the mood change—from the dizzy heights of joyous success to the gloomy pits of hideous doubt and self-hating in one hour. Rick tried to comfort, Rick tried to placate, Rick tried to reason. But how could I tell him that he was part of the problem? That he was a nice guy to talk to but I didn't particularly want him or his Nikons or his hopelessly romantic notions along on my trip. I can deal with pigs so easily, but nice people always confound me. How can you tell a nice person that you wish they were dead, that they'd never been born, that you wish they would crawl away into some hole and expire? No, not that, merely that you wish fate had never caused you to meet. In retrospect, I should never have allowed myself to see Rick as a fellow human being at all. I should always have regarded him as a necessary machine without feelings, a camera in fact. But I didn't. Rick was part and parcel of my trip willy-nilly and I kicked myself for allowing it to happen. I should have laid down the law then and there. I should have said, "Rick, you may come out three times for three or four days at a stretch and I want you involved in this thing as little as possible and that's that." But as usual I let the situation play itself out. I allowed my brain and will to put off till tomorrow what should have been done today, and said nothing.

Rick had not been through the preparations, did not comprehend what had gone before, did not perceive that I was as feeble a human being as any other, did not understand why I wanted to do it, and therefore projected his own emotional needs on to the trip. He was caught up in the romance of the thing— the magic—a side-effect I had not expected, but one which I had seen in many people, even my close friends. And Rick wanted to record this great event, my traipsing from point A to point B. My mistake in choosing Rick became apparent to me. I should have chosen some hard calloused typical photographer whom I could be nasty, vicious and cruel to without a trace of conscience. Rick had an outstanding quality, apart from his practised lovableness, and that was his naïvety. A fragility, a kind of introverted sweetness and perceptiveness that is rare enough in men, and virtually unique in successful photographers. I liked him. And I realized that he needed this trip perhaps as much as I did. And that was the burden. Instead of getting away from all responsibility to people, I was obviously heading straight into a heavy one. And I felt robbed.

Robyn's father, Mark Davidson
(left), had walked across Africa in
his youth and may have come closest
to understanding the forces that
were drawing his daughter into the
desert. Sallay (middle) made Robyn
a traditional pack saddle.

*T*HE CHEQUE ARRIVED. I SET A DEPARTURE DATE. I COMMISSIONED A TRADITIONAL Afghani pack saddle from Sallay. I bought equipment and food. My family wrote saying they would come out and say goodbye. People gave me gifts for the journey and everyone, everyone, seemed to be involved in a mounting excitement. As if we all suddenly believed it was true, that I was actually going to do it, after having just played a two-year game of pretend, or as if we had participated together in a dream, and had just woken up to find it real. The preparations had been, in a sense, the most important part of the event. From the day the thought came into my head "I am going to enter a desert with camels" to the day I felt the preparations to be completed, I had built something intangible but magical for myself which had rubbed off a little on to other people, and I would probably never have the opportunity to do anything as demanding or as fulfilling as that ever again.

I had given myself a week in Alice to tidy up all last-minute details. That involved getting together in one enormous pile all my fifteen hundred pounds of baggage, picking up the saddle from Sallay and seeing if it fitted, and buying all the perishable foodstuffs.

It also meant spending a week with my family, whom I hadn't seen in over a year, and arranging with Rick when I would see him on the track and how, and saying countless goodbyes. In short, it was one hell of a hectic week.

Rick came laden with every trapping under the sun. The people from whom he had bought his four-wheel-drive Toyota in Melbourne had seen him coming a mile off. "Hey, boys, here's a live one." They had sold him every survival gadget they had, from a winch the size of a bull to a rubber dinghy with paddles that took a half an hour to inflate.

"Rick, what on earth... what's THAT for?"

"Well, they told me it might flash flood out here, so I thought I'd better get it. I don't know. I've never been in a desert before."

We were at Sallay's, and after we picked ourselves off the ground where we had been rolling convulsed and pointing at Rick, we teased him unmercifully.

He had also bought me a two-way radio, and a huge gleaming contraption that looked like a chrome-plated exercise bicycle that plump people use.

"Richard, I'm going to be walking twenty miles a day. Why would I need an exercise bicycle?"

I didn't want a two-way radio, and I definitely didn't want this stationary bike either. It was for generating power, should the batteries fail on the radio. Imagine sitting out in the middle of nowhere, pedalling as hard as you could saying "help" into a microphone. I'd feel silly.

An argument ensued, with me saying that I refused to take either of these machines, and everyone else saying things like, "But you must," or "If you don't, I'll worry myself sick," or "Oh, my heart," or "What if you break a leg?" or "Please take it, Rob, for us. Just to make us feel better."

Emotional blackmail.

I had thought hard about a radio, and had decided it was somehow not right to take one. It didn't feel right. I didn't need it, didn't want to think of it sitting up there, tempting me, didn't want that mental crutch, or physical link with the outside world. Foolish I suppose, but it was a very strong feeling.

I gave in grudgingly to taking the set, but refused the pedal part point blank. I was angry with myself then, for allowing other people to stop me doing things the way I wanted to do them, for whatever reason. And angry because that other one of me, the boring practical self-preserver, had said, "Take it, take it, you idiot. You want to die out there or something?"

It was another tiny symbol of defeat. Of the trip not really being mine at all. I stashed it away with all the others.

Meanwhile, I watched my family. My father and sister. Between us, it seemed, there had always been invisible ropes and chains that we had chafed at, fought against, thought we had escaped from only to find them as strong as ever. We were bound together, since the death of my mother, by guilt and the overwhelming need to protect one another, mostly from ourselves. It was never stated between us. That would have been too cruel—the opening of old wounds. And, in fact, we had managed to bury it successfully, hide it behind set patterns of relating. And if sometimes one of us cracked with the pressure of it, we hastily explained it in terms that would not hurt, that would protect, that would cover up. But now a certain awareness pleaded from behind blue eyes, and begged for recognition in the set of three similar faces. It was like electricity. A need to lay a ghost, I suppose, before it was too late (i.e., before I karked in the desert). It was painful. We none of us wanted to make the

As dawn broke on the morning of the trip, Robyn feared, even after two years of preparation, that she still wasn't truly prepared for what lay ahead.

Words spoken when people think they may never see each other again are often stripped of pretense. Robyn and her father shared the sunrise together.

same mistake twice, of leaving too much unsaid, of not at least trying to state the unstateable.

My sister and I lived totally different kinds of lives at that stage. She was married with four children. We appeared on the surface as different as chalk and cheese, but we had that closeness that only two siblings who have shared a traumatic childhood can have. And it was between us that the conspiracy was strongest and most clearly stated and accepted. The need to protect Pop. The duty. To save him pain at any cost. It is odd that both of us spent most of our lives doing just the opposite.

And as I watched our reactions, as I saw his eyes mist over when he thought no one was looking, or glance away in confusion when he knew someone was, I got an inkling of just how much emotional charge was being focused on this trip. I began to see how much it meant to him and how much it would take out of him. Not just because he was proud of it. (He had spent twenty years in Africa, walking across it in the 1920s and 1930s, living the life of a Victorian explorer. He could now refer to me as a chip off the old block.) Nor simply because he was frightened. But because all the stupid meaningless pain our family had suffered might somehow be symbolically absolved, laid to rest through this gesture of mine. As if I could walk it away for all of us.

Sallay offered to truck the camels to Glen Helen, a spectacular red sandstone gorge, seventy miles west of Alice. That way, I'd miss the bitumen road, the tourists and the curious townsfolk. I arranged to meet him at the trucking yards at dawn on my last day. Pop and I rose at three a.m. to walk the camels down. It was still dark and we weren't talking much, just enjoying the moonlight and night noises, and each other's company.

After about half an hour of this he said, "You know, Rob, I had a strange dream about you and me last night." I could not remember Pop ever telling me anything as personal as a dream before. I knew it was difficult for him to talk like this. I put my arm around him. "Yes, what was it?"

"Well, we were sailing a lovely boat together on the

most beautiful tropical turquoise sea, and we were very happy, and we were going somewhere. I don't know where it was, but somewhere nice. And then suddenly, we were on a mud-bank, or a sea of mud rather, and you were so frightened. But I said to you, don't worry, darling, if we can float on water, we can float on mud."

I wondered if the dream meant the same to him as it did to me. It didn't matter, it was enough that he had told me. We hardly spoke again.

The night at Glen Helen was normal enough. Sallay cooked chapaties, Iris made us laugh, Pop and I went for walks, the kids had rides, my sister and brother-in-law wished they could spend more time out bush and Rick took pictures. To my surprise, the minute my head touched the swag I fell asleep.

But oh how different the dawning. We all woke up with tight forced smiles which soon enough disintegrated into covert then overt weeping. Sallay loaded the camels and I couldn't believe I had so much stuff, or that any of it would stay there. It was ridiculous. I could feel anxiety and excitement bulging the back of my eyeballs, and playing violins in my stomach. I knew they all had that sinking feeling that they would never see me alive again, and I had the sinking certainty that I would have to send messages from Redbank Gorge the same day, saying, "Sorry, muffed it on the first seventeen miles, please collect."

Josephine started bawling which started Andree which started Marg which started Pop, and there were hugs and good lucks and "Watch out for those bull camels like I told you," from Sallay, and feeble little pats on the back, and Marg looked deep into my eyes and said, "You know I love you, don't you," and Iris was waving and then everyone was waving, "Goodbye, sweetheart, goodbye, Rob," and I grabbed the nose-line with cold sweaty shaking hands, and walked up over the hill.

All around me was magnificence. Light, power, space and sun. And I was walking into it. I was going to let it make me or break me. A great weight lifted off my back. I felt like dancing and calling to the great spirit. Mountains pulled and pushed,

The last sight Robyn's friends and
family had of her was a simple
wave and the camel's packs disap-
pearing over the hill.

wind roared down chasms. I followed eagles suspended from cloud horizons. I wanted to fly in the unlimited blue of the morning. I was seeing it all as if for the first time, all fresh and bathed in an effulgence of light and joy, as if a smoke had cleared, or my eyes been peeled. I wanted to shout to the vastness, "I love you. I love you, sky, bird, wind, precipice, space sun desert desert desert."

Click.

"Hi, how's it goin'? I got some great shots of you waving goodbye." Rick had been sitting in his car, listening to Jackson Browne, waiting for me to come round the bend.

I had almost forgotten. I plummeted back to earth, my grandiose emotions crashing into shards of fussy practical detail. I looked at the camels. Dookie's pack was all skew-whiff. Zeleika was pulling at her nose-line to see where Goliath was and Goliath was straining at his rope which was pulling off Bub's saddle, trying to get to his mother.

Rick took hundreds of photos. At first I felt uncomfortable and camera-shy. And if one vain little voice said, "Don't show that gold filling when you smile," or "Watch those double chins," she was soon defeated by the sheer impossibility of remaining self-conscious in the face of the burgeoning quantity of film exposed. The camera seemed omnipresent. I tried to forget about it. I was almost successful. It wasn't that Rick was asking me to do anything, or interfering physically, it was just that he was there and his camera was recording images and giving them an isolated importance, which made my actions stilted and unspontaneous, as if I were just out of sync with myself. Click, observer. Click, observed. And whatever else could be said in their favour—cameras and Jackson Browne just didn't fit in this desert. I began right then and there to split into two over Rick. On the one hand I saw him as a blood-sucking little creep who had inveigled his way into my life by being nice and by tempting me with material things. On the other hand I was confronted with a very warm, gentle human being who genuinely wanted to help me and who was excited by the prospect of an adventure, who wanted to do a good job, and who cared.

Robyn headed down the road towards Areyonga.

*A*LL I REMEMBER OF THAT FIRST DAY ALONE WAS A FEELING OF release; a sustained buoyant confidence as I strolled along. Bub's nose-line in my sweaty palm, the camels in a well-behaved line behind me and Goliath bringing up the rear. The muffled tinkling of their bells, the soft crunching of my feet in the sand and the faint twittering of the wood-swallows were the only sounds. The desert was otherwise still.

I had decided to follow an abandoned track that would eventually meet up with the main Areyonga road. The definition of a track in Australia is a mark made across the landscape by the repeated passage of a vehicle or, if you are very lucky, initially by a bulldozer. These tracks vary in quality from a corrugated, bull-dust-covered, well-defined and well-used road to something which you can barely discern by climbing a hill and squinting in the general direction you think the said track may go. Sometimes you can see where a track is by the tell-tale blossoms of wildflow-ers. You may be able to follow the trail by searching for the ridge left eons ago by a bulldozer. The track may wind around or over hills and ridges and rocky outcroppings, straight into sand-dunes, get swallowed up by sandy creek-beds, get totally lost in stony creek-beds, or fray into a maze of animal pads. Following tracks is most often easy, sometimes frustrating, and occasionally downright terrifying.

When you are in cattle or sheep station country, the following of tracks can be especially puzzling, mainly because one always assumes that a track will lead somewhere. This is not necessarily so since station people just don't think like that. Also there is the problem of choice. When you are presented with half a dozen tracks all leading off in the general direction you want to go, all used within the last year, and none of them marked on the map, which one do you choose? If you choose the wrong one it may simply stop five miles ahead, so that you have to back-track, having lost half a day's travel. Or it may lead you to an aban-doned, waterless windmill and bore, or slap-bang into a new fence-line, which, if followed, will begin leading you in exactly the opposite direction to where you thought you wanted to go.

"The country I was travelling through held my undivided attention with its diversity. Contrary to popular belief, the desert is bountiful and teeming with life in the good seasons. It is like a vast untended communal garden, the closest thing to earthly paradise I can imagine."

Robyn's three adult camels carried the food, water, clothing and equipment necessary for her survival. Each morning she would load special metal water bags and 500 pounds of gear onto each animal. At night she would unload the 1500 pounds of gear once again.

However, that first day held none of these problems. If the track petered out into dust bowls with drinking spots in the middle of them, it was relatively easy to find where it continued on the other side. The camels were going well and behaving like lambs. Life was good.

I was a little nervous my first night out. Not because I was frightened of the dark (the desert is benign and beautiful at night, and except for the eight-inch-long, pink millipedes that sleep under the bottom of the swag and may wish to bite you at dawn, or the careless straying of a scorpion under your sleep-twitching hand, or the lonely slithering of a Joe Blake who may want to cuddle up and get warm under the bedclothes then fang you to death when you wake up, there is not too much to worry about) but because I wondered if I would ever see the camels again. I hobbled them out at dusk, unclogged their bells and tied little Goliath (yes, Zelly had given birth) to a tree. Would it work, I asked myself? The answer came back, "She'll be right, mate," the closest thing to a Zen statement to come out of Australia, and one I used frequently in the months ahead.

The process of unloading had been infinitely easier than putting the stuff on. It only took an hour. Then there was wood to be gathered, a fire and lamp to be lit, camels to be checked on, cooking utensils, food and cassette player to be got out, Diggity to be fed, camels to be checked on, food to be cooked and camels to be checked on. They were munching their heads off happily enough. Except Goliath. He was yelling piggishly for his mother, who, thank god, was taking no notice whatsoever.

I think I cooked a freeze-dried dish that night. The fruit was O.K., you could eat that straight like biscuit, but the meat and vegetable dishes were tasteless soggy tack. I fed all my packets to the camels later on, and stuck with what was to be my staple diet: brown rice, lentils, garlic, curry, oil, pancakes made with all manner of cereals and coconut and dried egg, various root vegetables cooked in the coals, cocoa, tea, sugar, honey, powdered milk, and every now and then, the ultimate in luxury, a can of sardines, some pepperoni and Kraft cheese, a tin of fruit,

Evening temperatures in the desert often dropped below freezing so a warm fire was a welcome way to end a hard day's work. After mak- *ing camp, Robyn would cook dinner and then listen to teaching tapes that taught her to speak Pitjantjara, the local aboriginal dialect.*

and an orange or lemon. I supplemented this with vitamin pills, various wild foods, and the occasional rabbit. Far from being deficient, this diet had me so healthy, I felt like a cast-iron amazon; cuts and gashes vanished in a day, I could see almost as well at night as in sunlight, and I grew muscles on my shit.

After that first lack-lustre meal, I built the fire up, checked on the camels, and put my Pitjantjara learning tapes into the cassette. Nyuntu palya nyinanyi. Uwa, palyarna, palu nyuntu, I mumbled repeatedly at the night sky now thick and gorgeous with billions of stars. There was no moon that night.

I nodded off with Diggity snoring in my arms as usual. And from that first night, I developed a habit of waking once or twice to check on the bells. I would wait until I heard a chime, and if I didn't I would call to them so they turned their heads and chimed, and if that didn't work, I would get up and see where they were. They were usually no more than a hundred yards from camp. I would then fall instantly back to sleep and remember waking up only vaguely in the morning. When I woke well before dawn, one fear at least had diminished. The camels were huddled around my swag, as close as they could get without actually crushing me.

My main problem now seemed to be whether the gear would hold together, whether the saddles would rub, and how the camels handled the work. I was a little worried over Zeleika. Diggity was doing fine but occasionally got footsore. I felt great, if knock-kneed with exhaustion by the end of a day. I decided to cover approximately twenty miles a day, six days a week. (And on the seventh she rested.) Well, not always. I wanted to keep a fair distance covered in case something went wrong, and I had to sit somewhere for days or weeks. There was a slight pressure on me not to take it as easy as I would have liked. I didn't want to be travelling in summer and I had promised *Geographic* I would be at journey's end before the year was out. That gave me six months of comfortable travel, which I could stretch to eight if needs be.

"YOU'VE LOST A WHOLE ROAD," I SAID TO MYSELF, INCREDULOUSLY. "NOT JUST A turning or a well or a ridge, but a whole bloody road. Take it easy, babe, be calm, she'll be right, mate, settle down settle DOWN."

My little heart felt like a macaw in a canary cage. I could feel the enormity of the desert in my belly and on the back of my neck. I was not in any real danger. I could easily have set a compass course for Areyonga. But I kept thinking, what if this happens when I'm two hundred miles from anywhere? What if, what if. And I felt very small and very alone suddenly in this great emptiness. I could climb a hill and look to where the horizon shimmered blue into the sky and see nothing. Absolutely nothing.

I re-read the map. No enlightenment there. I was only fifteen or so miles from the settlement, and here was this giant dirt highway where there should only be sandstone and roly-poly. Should I follow it or what? Was it a new mining road? I checked the map for mines but there was nothing marked.

I sat back and watched myself perform. "O.K. First of all, you are not lost, you are merely misplaced, no no, you know exactly where you are so stifle that impulse to scream at the camels and kick Diggity. Think clearly. Then, make camp for the night here, there is plenty of green feed, and spend the rest of the afternoon looking for that goddamn track. If you don't find it, cut across country. Easy enough. Above all, do not flap around like a winged pigeon. Where's your pride? Right."

I did all that, then went off scouting, map in hand, Diggity at foot. I found an ancient trail that wound up through the mountains, not exactly where the map said it should be but close enough for a margin of credibility at least. It went for a couple of miles off course then came out to meet up with, yes, yet another major highway that had no right to exist. "Shit and damnation." This I followed for another half mile in the general direction of Areyonga, until I came across a bullet-ridden piece of tin bent over double and almost rusted away, but with an arrow that pointed at the ground and the letters A   ON   upon it. I skipped back to camp in the gathering twilight, apologized profusely to my poor dumb entourage, and fixed lesson one firmly in my brain for future reference. When in doubt, follow your nose, trust your instincts, and don't rely on maps.

I had been alone for three days in country that people seldom visited. Now I was crawling down a wide dusty deserted boring road, an occasional beer or coke can winking at me from the bushes. The walking was beginning to take its toll on all of us. Diggity's feet were pincushioned with bindy-eye prickles, so

I heaved her up on to Dookie's back. She hated it, and stared off into the distance, sighing dramatically, with that long-suffering look common to brainwashed dogs. My own feet were blistered and aching, and my legs cramped up as soon as I stopped walking. Zeleika had a large lump which distended her milk vein and her nose-peg was infected. Dookie's saddle was rubbing him slightly but he stepped high and seemed, unlike the others, to be thoroughly enjoying himself. I suspected he had always wanted to travel.

I arrived a mile outside Areyonga by mid-afternoon to be met by hordes of excited children giggling, shouting and raving Pitjantjara. God knows how they knew I was coming, but now, from Areyonga all the way down the line, the inexplicable communication network called "bush telegraph," or "keeping one's ear to the ground," would tell people I was on my way.

I had been hot, irritable and tired when I arrived, but now these delightful children lifted my spirits with their cacaphony of laughter. How easy they were. I had always felt slightly uncomfortable around most children, but Aboriginal kids were different. They never whined, whinged or demanded. They were direct and filled with joie de vivre and so loving and giving with one another that they melted me immediately. I tried out my Pitjantjara. Stunned silence, then hoots of laughter. I let them lead the camels. There were children on my back, children clinging to camel legs and camel saddles and children ten deep on every side. The camels had a very special attitude to them. They would let them do anything, so I didn't have to worry about anyone getting hurt. Bub especially adored them. I remember how, at Utopia, when he was tied to his tree during the day, he would see the kids bounding towards him after school, and would immediately sit down and start to doze off in pleasant expectation of being jumped on, bounced on, pulled, tugged, pushed and walked on by the small people. By the time I got to the village proper everyone was out to meet me, all asking questions in lingo because word had already spread that the kungka rama-rama (crazy woman) could speak it fluently. I could not. It didn't seem to matter.

The camels were like a key in relating to the Pitjantjara people. I could not have picked a better way to travel through their country. It was a stroke of genius. They had a special relationship with these animals as they had been the one tribe to use them constantly for walkabout right up to the mid-1960s, when cars and trucks took over. The whole of the first section of my trip would be through their tribal territory, or what was left of it, a large reserve controlled by white bureaucrats and dotted with mission and government settlements.

The camels took to travel and seemed to enjoy the sense of mission that Robyn imparted to the journey. They all grew used to the daily 20 mile rhythm and Robyn usually rode Bub. When he got through an entire day without being spooked, Robyn rewarded him with tasty plant snacks.

*W*HEN WE WERE ALL RESTED, WE HEADED OFF FOR TEMPE DOWNS STATION, forty-odd miles to the south, over an unused path through the ranges. I was a bit windy about my ability to navigate through these hills. The people at Areyonga had sapped my confidence by insisting that I call them on the two-way radio when I made it to the other side. No one had used the track for ten years and it would be invisible at times. The range itself was a series of mountains, chasms, canyons and valleys that ran all the way to Tempe, perpendicular to my direction of travel.

I set off clutching map and compass. Every hour or so, my shoulders would tighten and my stomach knot as I searched for the right path. I got lost only once, ending up in a box-canyon and having to back-track to where the path had been obliterated by a series of cattle and donkey tracks. But the constant tension was sapping my energy and I sweated and strained. This went on for two days.

One afternoon, after our midday break, something dropped off Bub's back and he flew into a flat panic. I now had Zeleika in the lead, because of her sore nose, and Bub at the rear. He bucked and he bucked and the more he bucked, the more bits of pack went flying and the more frenzied he became. By the time he stopped, the saddle was dangling under his quivering belly, and the goods were scattered everywhere. I switched into automatic. The other camels were ready to leap out of their skins and head for home. Goliath was galloping between them and generally causing havoc. There was not a tree in sight to tie them to. If I blew this, they might take off and I would never see them again. I couldn't get back to Bub so I whooshed the lead camel down and tied her nose-line to her foreleg, so that if she tried to get up, she would be pulled down. I did the same with Dook, clouted Goliath across the nose with a branch of mulga so that he took off in a cloud of dust, and then went back to Bub. His eyes had rolled with fear and I had

One day, after hanging up some sheets and blankets to air in the morning breeze, Robyn saw something wraithlike at the corner of her field of vision and swung around with a rush of adrenaline. It was the first time she realized how easy it was for the camels to see spooky ghosts behind every bush.

to talk to him and pacify him until I knew he trusted me and wouldn't kick.

Then I lifted the saddle with my knees and undid the girth on top of his back. Then I gently took it off and whooshed him down like the others. I found a tree a little further on, and beat the living daylights out of him. The whole operation had been quick, sure, steady and precise, like Austrian clockwork—perfect. But now, whatever toxins had been stirred up by the flow of adrenalin hit my bloodstream like the Cayuhogan River. I lay by the tree, trembling as hard as Bub. I had been out of control when I beat him and began to recognize a certain

Unlike horses, camels can bend
their legs and actually kneel to get
up and down. Robyn would
command them in Arabic learned
from Sallay, "Arrah!" and with
tremendous grace they would lift
their hindquarters, rise up on their
front legs and off they'd go.

Kurtishness in my behavior. This weakness, my inability to be terrified with any dignity, came to the forefront often during the trip, and my animals took the brunt of it. If, as Hemingway suggested, "courage is grace under pressure," then the trip proved once and for all that I was sadly lacking in the stuff. I felt ashamed.

I learnt a couple of other things from that incident. I learnt to conserve energy by allowing at least part of myself to believe I could cope with any emergency. And I realized that this trip was not a game. There is nothing so real as having to think about survival. It strips you of airy-fairy notions. Believing in omens and fate is all right as long as you know exactly what you are doing. I was becoming very careful and I was coming right back down to earth, where the desert was larger than I could comprehend.

And not only was space an ungraspable concept, but my description of time needed reassessment. I was treating the trip like a nine-to-five job. Up bright and early (oh, the guilt if I slept in), boil the billy, drink tea, hurry up it's getting late, nice place for lunch but I can't stay too long...I simply could not rid myself of this regimentation. I was furious with myself, but I let it run its course. Better to watch it now, then fight it later when I was feeling stronger. I had a clock which I told myself was for navigation purposes only, but at which I stole furtive glances from time to time. It played tricks on me. In the heat of the afternoon, when I was tired, aching and miserable, the clock would not move, hours lapsed between ticks and tocks. I recognized a need for these absurd arbitrary structures at that stage. I did not know why, but I knew I was afraid of something like chaos. It was as if it were waiting for me to let down my guard and then it would pounce.

On the third day, and to my great relief, I found the well-used station track to Tempe. I called Areyonga on my radio set, that unwanted baggage, that encumbrance, that infringement of my privacy, that big smudgy patch on the purity of my gesture. I screamed into it that I was all right and got nothing but static as a reply.

One of Robyn's hopes was that Diggity would learn to track the camels if they disappeared during the night. But things didn't quite work out that way. "Diggity's desire to hunt everything except camels was a bone of contention between us. I had been trying to train her to help me track them but she was not remotely interested. Her all-consuming passions were kangaroos and rabbits and these she would chase for hours on end, bounding over clumps of spinifex, head turning this way and that in mid-air like Nureyev. She was beautiful to watch but never actually caught anything."

$\mathcal{B}$Y THE TIME I GOT NEAR WALLERA RANCH, TWO DAYS AFTER Tempe, the tourists were driving me crazy. In overrigged vehicles they came in droves to see Ayers Rock, Australia's natural wonder. They had two-way radios, winches, funny hats with corks on them, stubbies (beer bottles) and leather stubbie-holders with emus, kangaroos and naked women tooled upon them, all this to travel down a perfectly safe road. And they had cameras. I sometimes think tourists take cameras with them because they feel guilty about being on holiday, and feel they should be doing something useful with their time. In any case, when otherwise perfectly nice people don their hats and become tourists, they change into bad-mannered, loud, insensitive, litter-bugging oafs.

I must make a distinction here between travellers and tourists. I did meet some lovely people on the road, but they were rarer than hen's teeth. At first I treated one and all with pleasant politeness. There were ten questions invariably asked me, and I unfailingly gave my pat reply. I posed for the inevitable snap snap of Nikons and whirr of Super-eights. It got so that I was stopped every half hour and by three in the afternoon, the dangerous hour for me, a time when my senses of humour and perspective fail me badly, a time I cannot even be nice to myself, let alone these fools who would pile out, block my path, frighten the camels, hold me up, ask stupid questions, capture me on celluloid so that they could stick me on their refrigerator doors when they got home, or worse still, sell me to newspapers when the heat was on, then drive off in a cloud of choking blinding dust, not even offering me a drink of water—by three in the afternoon I would begin to get mean. My rudeness made me feel a little better but not much. The best policy was simply to keep off the road or feign deafness.

Those two weeks were strangely disappointing. The

The tourists Robyn encountered
along the way were a constant
source of irritation. They frightened
her camels by zooming up along

side and many were downright
rude to Robyn as well, gawking at
her without even offering her a
drink of water.

initial buzz had worn off and little niggling doubts were starting to worm their way into my consciousness. I was feeling ambiguous about it all. Nothing portentous or grand was really happening to me. I had been expecting some miraculous obvious change to occur. It was all nice of course and even fun sometimes, but hey, where was the great clap of the thunder of awareness that, as everyone knows, knocks people sideways in deserts. I was exactly the same person that I was when I began.

Some camps on those nights were so desolate they stole into my soul. I longed for a safe nook out of that chill empty wind. I felt vulnerable. Moonlight turned shadows into inimical forms and I was so glad of Diggity's warmth as we snuggled beneath the blankets that I could have squeezed her to death. The rituals I performed provided another necessary structure. Everything was done correctly and obsessionally. Before I went to bed, everything was placed exactly where I wanted it for the morning. Before the trip I had been hopelessly vague, forgetful and sloppy. My friends had made cracks about how I would probably forget to take the camels one morning. Now it was the opposite. The food was packed away, billy filled with water, tea, cup, sugar and Thermos out, nose-lines on the tree. I would roll out the swag, just so, by the fire and study my star book.

Stars all made sense to me now that I lived under them. They told me the time when I awoke at night for a piss and a check on the bells. They told me where I was and where I was going, but they were cold like bits of frost. One night, I decided to listen to some music and put Eric Satie into the cassette. But the noise sounded alien, incongruous, so I turned it off and sucked on the whisky bottle instead. I talked to myself, rolling the names of the stars and constellations around my tongue. Goodnight, Aldebaran. See you, Sirius. Adios, Corvus.

Wallera Ranch was not a ranch at all but a watering-hole for tourists. I went into the bar for a beer, there to be met by a group of typical ockers, all talking, as is their wont, about sex and sheilas. "Oh great," I thought, "just what I need. Some intellectual stimulation." I left.

Many of the tourists who accosted
Robyn would snap pictures, pester
her with questions, or treat her
like an outback sideshow. Their

behavior reminded her that
Aborigines wisely divide people into
two groups: tourists and travellers.

Uluru

And then I saw the thing. I was thunderstruck. I could not believe that blue form was real. It floated and mesmerized and shimmered and looked too big. It was indescribable.

The indecipherable power of that rock had my heart racing. I had not expected anything quite so weirdly, primevally beautiful.

The great monolithic rock was surrounded by fertile flats for a radius of half a mile which, because of the added run-off water, were covered in lush green feed and wildflowers so thick you couldn't step between them. Then the dunes began, radiating away as far as the eye could see, orange fading into dusty blue.

I sat up on the first sandhill watching the gathering evening changing the bold harsh daylight colours to luminous pastels, then deeper to the blues and purples of peacock feathers. This was always my favourite time of day in that country—the light, which has a crystalline quality I have not seen in any other place, lingers for hours. The Rock did not disappoint me, far from it. All the tourists in the world could not destroy it, it was too immense, too forceful, too ancient to be corruptible.

There were very few of the Pitjantjara mob left here. Most had moved away to more private tribal areas, though a few remained to protect and look after what is an extremely important site in their mythic culture. They were making a meagre living by selling artefacts to the tourists. Uluru they called it. The great Uluru. I wondered how they could stand watching people blundering around in fertility caves, or climbing the white painted line up the side, and taking their endless photos. If it had me almost to the point of tears, how much more must it have meant to them. There was one miserably smalled fenced-off section on the western side which read, "Keep out. Aboriginal sacred site."

*I*T DID NOT HELP THAT THE MAGAZINE HAD INSISTED THAT RICK GET NEW AND exciting shots of the Rock. I posed in caves and walked back and forth across sand-dunes. I led the camels over escarpments and I rode them through wildflowers. "What about honest journalism?" I shouted, and set my face into cement-like grimaces as I stamped along. Poor Richard, how I made him pay. I think he was truly frightened of me at times. But he was certainly game. I put him on Dookie for a ride, while I rode Bub, who started to shy and pig-root. I yelled at Richard to hang on, but through the fracas, I could hear the steady clicking of his camera. I have noticed this trait in many photographers—the ability to be much braver when they are looking through a lens than when they are not.

I had been looking forward to seeing the Olgas for years now. They were the sisters to Ayers Rock, and they looked like great red loaves of bread that some giant had dropped out of the sky. From the Rock, they were a cluster of lavender pebbles along the horizon. I wanted to spend a few days there, away from the tourists, wandering, exploring and just enjoying the lack of pressure, and the time to myself so I could sit and think and sort out my tangles, without worrying about having to get somewhere, or be concerned for anyone else. I wanted to get away again, recapture that feeling of freedom that I had thought would be permanent when I left Redbank Gorge. It was not to be.

I walked the twenty miles through country that should have mended me but which I did not allow even to penetrate. I was depressed. I felt cheated and put upon, and my face looked like a viola. I hated Rick and blamed him for everything. Besides, he didn't like the desert, couldn't see it. He didn't belong and he couldn't light fires, or cook, or fix trucks. He was like a fish out of water and he thought the countryside boring. He would listen to music or read until I came into view, then he would take his photos using the magnificent earth as a backdrop.

The other difficulty was that, while my reaction to tension is to let it build up then explode it away in a fit of fury, Rick's was to sulk. I had never met such a terminal sulker. I would rather he had hit me than sulked because I couldn't stand it. By the end of the day I would practically grovel at his feet in an effort to get him to talk, or fight, or something. Anything. And Diggity adored him. "Betraying brat," I thought, "and you usually have such good taste in people."

We arrived at the Olgas that night in a tight silence, and set up camp

directly beneath them. They glowed orange, then red, then iridescent pink, then purple, then turned into a black cut-out against glowing moonlight. Rick called the ranger at Ayers Rock, to test his radio, but not only could he not contact him, a mere twenty miles away, but he had a crackly conversation with a fisherman in Adelaide, five hundred miles to the south.

'Oh wonderful. Wonderful. Just as well we brought radio sets, eh, Rick? I mean when I'm bleeding and croaking out in the middle of woop-woop, a mile from the nearest station, it's nice to know I can always have a pleasant chat to someone in Alaska. Wouldn't you agree, Richard? Richard?'

Richard remained silent.

That night I couldn't stand any more. I grabbed Rick by the hand, sat him down beside me by the fire and said: "O.K., mate, you win. I can't take any more. We'll have to work something out because this is just plain ridiculous. Here we are in the middle of a most magical desert, involved in something which should be giving us joy, and we're acting like children."

Richard continued staring into the fire, a stricken look around his eyes, and his bottom lip protruding, just a fraction. I tried again.

"It's like this story about the two monks you know. They're not allowed to have anything to do with women. Anyway, they're walking along together and they see this woman drowning out in a stream. And one monk jumps into the water and carries her to the bank. Then they keep on

It took Robyn an entire day to make the 20 mile trek from Uluru to the Olgas. Known to the aborigines as "Katatjuta," which means "place of many heads," the Olgas are composed of 36 round rock domes.

walking for a while in silence and suddenly the second monk can't hold it back any more and he says, 'How could you touch that woman?' And the first monk looks up surprised and answers, 'Oh, are you still carrying the woman?' Well you see what I mean, Richard, we're both the second dumb monk and it's stupid and destructive and it's driving me to drink. I've got enough to worry about, and life is too short to treat like a dress rehearsal. So, either you leave right now, I send the money back to *Geographic* and we forget the whole thing, or we reach some better understanding of what we both want and how to go about getting it. O.K.?"

We talked. We talked for hours and hours about every subject under the sun, ending up laughing and being friends which was a great relief.

I had also said he could come along with me to Docker River, five days away, and although I desperately wanted to be on my own again, it seemed churlish to send him away, given that he wanted to get photographs of Aborigines, and this would probably be one of the few places he could do so. Although I felt disturbed by this prospect (I knew Aboriginal people were thoroughly sick of having lenses stuck up their nostrils by insensitive tourists), I thought that any press coverage they could get, at this stage in their demise, would be a good thing, providing it was done with their consent.

I did not perceive at that time that I was allowing myself to get more involved with an article about the trip than the trip itself. It did not dawn on me that already I was beginning to see it as a story for other people, with a beginning and an ending.

Then the rain came. Great angry thundering clouds swarmed and bustled out of nowhere, and it hailed and poured a deluge. It rained cats and dogs, elephants and whales, and I stumbled through it, cold and wet and holding my anger to me like a baby. I was worried as usual over the camels. And I was exhausted. Exhausted by the work and worry, exhausted by the anger, and exhausted by my thoughts, which went round and round in circles, always returning to the central fact that I was involved in a pointless ludicrous farce.

And of course that was the night that dear little Goliath decided he didn't like being caught and tied to a tree any more. I chased him for over an hour at a run. I entered a new realm of exhaustion. I was covered with freezing mud,

By tying up Goliath every night, Robyn assured that Zelly (and therefore the "boys" who always followed Zelly's lead) would be around in the morning. The key was catching Goliath when it was time to make camp for the night. One evening Goliath, who now weighed over 200 pounds, decided he no longer liked being caught or tied up.

$\mathcal{W}$E WERE A DAY OR TWO SHORT OF DOCKER, WHEN THE FIRST MAJOR DISASTER of the trip occurred. I was carefully leading my camels through a river that had once been a track, when Dookie, the last in line, slipped and landed flat in the water. I went back to him and asked him to stand up. I tapped him behind the shoulder and asked him again. He looked at me pitifully and groaned to his feet. The rain was blinding me and running down me in cold torrents. He could hardly use his front right leg.

We camped that day in a deep luminous glassy green light. I had no idea what was wrong with the leg. I prodded, rubbed and examined from shoulder to foot. It was tender but there was no swelling that I could see. I made hot compresses but did not know what else I could do. Was it a broken bone, a torn ligament, what? The point was that Dookie could not walk. He sat in the creek-bed miserable, and refused to move. I cut him feed and brought it to him and massaged the shoulder again. I hugged him, fussed over him, and all the while I felt sick and tired and beaten. A thought was invading me which I tried to keep away. That I might have to shoot my boy, that the trip might be ended, that it was all just a stupid pathetic joke. I was glad Richard was there.

At last, the rains cleared. Everything was rinsed clean and sparkling. We rested two days, then limped into Docker, where as usual there were hundreds of excited children to meet us. The community adviser gave us a caravan to live in, and Rick decided to stay until we knew what Dookie's fate would be. In the end I waited there six weeks, not knowing whether the leg would heal or not. Rick stayed for two. It was not a happy time.

It is amazing to me how human beings can remain calm, controlled and sensible on the surface, when internally they are cracking up, crumbling, breaking down. I can see now that that time in Docker was the beginning of a kind of mental collapse, though I could not have described it in such a way then. I was still functioning after all. The whites there were kind and did their best to entertain and look after me, but they could not know that I needed all my energy just to remain in that caravan and lick my wounds. They could not know that they were gutting me with their invitations that I was too morally weak to resist, that my endless smiles hid an overwhelming despair. I wanted to hide, I slept for hour after hour and when I woke up it was into nothingness. Grey nothingness. I was ill.

Whatever justifications for photographing the Aborigines I had come up with before, now were totally shot. It was immediately apparent that they hated

Sometimes it was safer to walk than ride. The bottom of a camel's foot is covered with a smooth pad like a bald tire. These pads contain a squishy, elastic sort of bladder that allows the camel to glide effortlessly over and through the sand. On treacherous surfaces like a rain-soaked creek bed these pads become very slippery. Without anywhere to hide from the downpour, Robyn and the camels carefully headed towards Docker River.

On the way to Docker River during this rainstorm Dookie slipped and crashed to the ground.

it. They knew it was a rip-off. I wanted Rick to stop. He argued that he had a job to do. I looked through a small booklet *Geographic* had given him to record expenditures. In it was "gifts to the natives." I couldn't believe it. I told him to put down five thousand dollars for mirrors and beads, then hand out the money. I also realized that coverage in a conservative magazine like *Geographic* would do the people no good at all, no matter how I wrote the article. They would remain quaint primitives to be gawked at by readers who couldn't really give a damn what was happening to them. I argued with Rick that he was involved in a form of parasitism, and besides, since everyone saw him as my husband, whatever they felt for him, they felt for me too. They were polite and deferential as always, and they took me hunting and food-gathering, but the wall was always there. He came up with all the old arguments, but was torn, I knew, because he recognized it was true.

It was coming time for him to leave and he felt thwarted—he had not done his job. One night we had heard wailing from down at camp. Without my knowledge, he snuck out of the caravan early the next morning and went down there to take pictures. He was not to know that he was recording a secret ceremony and sacred business, but he was lucky he didn't get a spear through his leg. I did not know this until after he had gone, but I could feel the people set against us. Not overtly, never overtly, but it was there, a feeling, which I thought was

simply because they could see through me. It seemed that one of my main aims, to be with Aboriginal people, was now unattainable.

Glenys, a nurse working for the Aboriginal health service, arrived a few days later. I immediately liked her. We went out often, hunting with the women, digging for maku (witchetty grub) and honey-ant and going on bunny bashes, in which the women find a warren, dig deep down into the earth with their crowbars and extract, if they're lucky, handfuls of rabbits, who then have their necks expertly cricked, and are slung on the back of the truck to be taken home and roasted in the coals. I loved these expeditions—twenty women and children would cram into and on to the Toyota, all laughing and talking, and we would drive thirty-odd miles to a special place.

Glenys and I decided to drive to Giles, a weather station one hundred miles west. There was a large Aboriginal camp there and a handful of whites to run the station. When we got to camp, we went and had a talk with some women. After a while, there was some whispering and conferring going on amongst them. An old lady then came up and asked us if we would like to learn to dance. Of course the answer was yes. We were led to a clearing away from the view of the camp. The oldest women, beautifully ugly old hags, squatted down at the front while the younger women and girls formed a mass behind them. Glenys and I sat in front. There was much touching and laughing and reassurance. I did not speak enough Pitjantjara to understand all they were saying, but it didn't matter. The mood was transmitted. Then the chanting began. It was led by the old ladies, different ones leading at different times. Others found sticks and tapped them one upon the other on the red earth in rhythm. I didn't know whether to join in, did not know the rules of conduct. But as it went on, that droning, dust-woven, meditative music, I felt transported and close to tears. The sound seemed to rise from the ground. It belonged so perfectly, it was a song of unity and recognition, and the old crones were like extensions of the earth. I wanted to understand so much. Why were they doing this for us, these smiling women? I melted into a feeling of belonging. They were letting me into their world. They asked me if I wanted to dance. I felt stupid and clumsy and afraid to get up.

Robyn urged Dookie to stand after his fall, but he obviously couldn't. He just lay there.

Eventually an old woman took me by the hand and to the strange clicking rhythm and the droning melody, she danced and made me copy her. I tried my best. There were hoots of laughter from behind. Tears rolled down faces and sides were clenched in a delight of laughter. I laughed with them, and my old teacher hugged me. She showed me again the difficult bodily tremor that came at the end of each cadence. At last I got it and then we danced in earnest, hopping and shuffling in grooves in the dust, and shaking at the end, and turning and going back and then slowly skipping in a circle. Hours passed. Gradually an unspoken group decision that the dance had ended thinned out the women. Soon everyone was moving away. We stood there, not knowing what was expected of us. We were about to leave too when one of the old women came up to us, puckered her toothless mouth, and said, "Six dollar you got six dollar." Her knobbly old hand was outstretched, the others turned and watched. I was dumbfounded, speechless. I had not thought… I gathered my speech and told her we didn't have any. I emptied my pockets to show her. "Two dollar, you got two dollar." Glenys fumbled and gave her all the change she had. I promised her I would send her the money, then my friend and I left.

We didn't talk much on the way home. I did not know then that it was merely a rule of etiquette to give some little gift at the end of a dance. I felt it as a symbolic defeat. A final summing up of how I could never enter their reality, would always be a whitefella tourist on the outside looking in.

And so it dragged on, that gradual decaying of my little hopes and dreams. While Dookie's shoulder began slowly to heal (I had diagnosed it by then as a torn muscle), I asked around Docker if any of the old men would like to come with me to Pipalyatjara. I wanted to cut across country for the next hundred and some-odd miles, but knew this would be through sacred country, dotted with sacred sites where women were not allowed to go. I could not do it without an old man. It would be the worst form of trespassing, but I desperately wanted to get away from the tracks. Without actually saying yes, they didn't say no either, a common form of politeness amongst Aborigines called courtesy bias. I knew they didn't trust me, even though I had no camera. I had found out from the irate community

adviser what Rick had done, knew that I was an accomplice and found it hard to look at them. Taking photos of secret business was far worse than desecrating a church could be to the staunchest of Christians. The Aborigines there sorted travellers into two sections, tourists and people; I realized that to them I had become a tourist.

There were only half a dozen whites at Docker. They were good people. From the community adviser to the mechanics to the store managers, they invited me to barbecues, on picnics and out hunting, but they could not penetrate my gloom.

By the time I was ready to leave, it was decided that none of the old men wanted to come. That meant 160 miles of dirt track, which, although I could expect to see no vehicles, I did not look forward to. I didn't know whether to continue. It all seemed rather pointless. I had sold the trip, misunderstood and mismanaged everything. I could not be with the Aboriginal people without being a clumsy intruder. The journey had lost all meaning, lost all its magical inspiring quality, was an empty and foolish gesture. I wanted to give up. But to do what? Go back to Brisbane? If this, the hardest and most worthwhile thing I had ever attempted, was a miserable failure, then what on earth would succeed? I left Docker, more unhappy, more negative, more weakened than I had ever been.

The day after Dookie's fall, Robyn spent hours painfully picking a desert plant that the camels loved because, like many prickly plants, it has a high water content. The prickles didn't bother Dookie's leatherlike tongue, but Robyn's hands were left torn and bloody.

Following pages: As was true everywhere she went, the aboriginal children greeted Robyn with tremendous excitement.

An Undeclared War

After 160 years of undeclared war on Aboriginal people, during which time wholesale slaughter was carried out in the name of progress, and while the last brutal massacre was taking place in the Northern Territory in 1930, the colonialist government set up Aboriginal reserves on land neither the cattlemen nor anyone else wanted. Because everyone believed that the indigenous people would eventually die out, allowing them to keep small sections of their land was seen as a temporary measure which would make life safer for the settlers. The blacks were rounded up like cattle by police and citizens on horseback wielding guns. Often, different tribes were forced to live on one small area; as some of these groups were traditionally antagonistic, this created friction and planted the seeds of cultural decay. The government allowed missionaries to rule many of these reserves and to confine and control the people. Half-caste children were taken forcibly from their mothers and kept separate, as they were seen as having at least a chance of becoming human.

Even these pitifully inadequate reserves are now under threat, because large mining concerns, have their eyes on them for further exploitation. Already, many companies have been allowed to mine what was once Aboriginal territory, bulldozing it into a scarred dust-bowl and leaving the people destitute, their land destroyed. Many reserves have been closed down and the people sent to the towns where they cannot find work. Although this is called "promoting assimilation", it is another method of transferring Aboriginal land to white ownership. However, Pitjantjara people are slightly better off than most other central desert and

northern tribes, because uranium has not yet been mined in their country and because the area is so remote. Many of the old people do not speak English, and the people on the whole have managed to keep their cultural integrity intact. It also became apparent to me that the majority of whites now involved with the Aborigines are fighting alongside them to protect what is left of their lands and their rights, and eventually to reach the point where the blacks are autonomous. Whether this is possible, given the rural white backlash, the racist attitudes of Australians generally and the genocidal policies of the present government, and given that the rest of the world seems neither to know nor care what is happening to the oldest culture in the world, is a doubtful question. The Aborigines do not have much time. They are dying.

I WAS ABOUT TO TURN OFF AND MAKE CAMP WHEN THROUGH THE HAZED AFTERNOON heat came striding three large strong male camels in full season.

Panic and shake. Panic and shake. They attack and kill, remember. Remember now, one—tie up Bub securely, two—whoosh him down, three—take rifle from scabbard, four—load rifle, five—cock, aim and fire rifle. They were just thirty yards away and one was spurting a cylindrical arch of red blood. He didn't seem to notice. They all came forward again.

I was scared deep in my bones. First, I could not believe it was happening, then I believed it was never going to stop. My ears thumped, cold sweat stuck to the hollow of my back. My vision was distorted by fear. Then I was past it, not thinking any more, just doing it.

Zzzt. This time just behind his head and he turned and ambled away. Zzzt. Near the heart again, he slumped down but just sat there. Zzzt. In the head, dead. The other two trundled off into the scrub. Shake and sweat, shake and sweat. You've won for now.

I unsaddled the camels and hobbled them close, glancing around constantly. It was getting dark. They came back. Braver now, I shot one. Wounded it. Night came too quickly.

The fire flickered on white moonstruck sand, the sky was black onyx. The rumbling sound of bulls circled the camp very close until I fell asleep. In the moonlight, I woke up and maybe twenty yards away was a beast standing in full profile. I loved it and didn't want to harm it. It was beautiful, proud. Not interested in me at all. I slept again, drifting off to the sound of bells on camels.

Came dawn, I was already stalking, gun loaded and ready. They were both still there. I had to kill the wounded one. I tried to. Another cylinder of blood and he ran away nipping at his wound. I could not follow. I knew he would die slowly but I could not follow, I had my own survival to think of. There he was, the last young bull, a beautiful thing, a moonlight camel. I made a decision. This one of the three would be allowed to live until he did something direct to jeopardize my safety. Happy decision. "Yes, maybe he'll tag along right to Carnarvon. And I'll call him Aldebaran and isn't he magnificent, Diggity, what a match for Dookie. I don't have to kill him at all." I snuck around to catch the camels. He watched me. Now, last camel to catch, Bub. Off he galloped in his hobbles, the new bull pacing lazily beside him. I couldn't catch him with the other bull so close. I tried for an hour, I was exhausted. I wanted to kill Bubby, to dismember him, rip his balls out, but they'd already gone. I took the rifle and I walked to within thirty feet of the now excited and burbling young bull. I put a slug right where I knew it would kill him. It did not, and he bit and roared at his wound. He didn't understand this pain, I was crying. I fired again into his head and he sat down, gurgling through his own blood. I walked up to his head, we stared at one another—he knew then. He looked at me, I shot him in the brain, point blank.

111

*T*HE COUNTRY WAS DRY. HOW COULD THE CAMELS BE SO THIRSTY and thin. At night, they came into camp and tried to knock over the water drums. I hadn't enough to spare. I rationed them. The map said "rockhole." Thank god. I turned off the track somewhere in that haze of elastic time and walked in. More sandhills, then a stretch of gibberflat, wide and dry and desolate with one dead bird, and two empty holes. Some string somewhere inside me was starting to unravel. An important string, the one that held down panic. I walked on. That night I camped in those sandhills...

The sky was leaden and thick. All day it had been grey, smooth, translucent, like the belly of a frog. Spots of rain spattered on me but not enough to lay the dust. The sky was washing me out, emptying me. I was cold as I hunched over my meagre fire. And somewhere, between frozen sandhills in a haunted and forgotten desert, where time is always measured by the interminable roll of constellations, or the chill call of a crow waking, I lay down on my dirty bundle of blankets. The frost clung like brittle cobwebs to the black bushes around me, while the sky turned thick with glitter. It was very still. I slept. The hour before the sun spills thin blood colour on the sand, I woke suddenly, and tried to gather myself from a dream I could not remember. I was split. I woke into limbo and could not find myself. There were no reference points, nothing to keep the

‖▽△▽△▽△▽△▽△▽△▽△▽△▽△‖

Sometimes Robyn's moods were internal reflections of the dry, dusty and hopeless landscape which seemed to have no beginning and no end.

world controlled and bound together. There was nothing but chaos and the voices.

The strong one, the hating one, the powerful one was mocking me, laughing at me.

"You've gone too far this time. I've got you now and I hate you. You're disgusting, aren't you. You're nothing. And I have you now, I knew it would come, sooner or later. There's no use fighting me you know, there's no one to help you. I've got you, I've got you."

Another voice was calm and warm. She commanded me to lie down and be calm. She instructed me to not let go, not give in. She reassured me that I would find myself again if I could just hold on, be quiet and lie down.

The third voice was screaming.

Diggity woke me at dawn. I was some distance from camp, cramped, and cold to my bones. The sky was cold, pale blue and pitiless, like an Austrian psychopath's eyes. I walked out into the time warp again. I was only half there, like an automaton. I knew what I had to do. "You must do this, this will keep you alive. Remember." I walked out into that evil whispering sea. Like an animal, I sensed a menace, everything was quite still, but threatening, icy, beneath the sun's heat. I felt it watching me, following me, waiting for me.

I tried to conquer the presence with my own voice. It croaked out into the silence and was swallowed by it. "All we have to do," it said, "is reach Mount Fanny, and there is certain to be water there. Just one step and another, that's all I have to do, I must not panic." I could see

One morning cheeky Bub decided
to sample Robyn's breakfast and she
scolded him for his impertinence.
A simple finger pointed to his nosepeg
had the same effect as actually
pulling on his string.

what had to be Mount Fanny in the hot blue distance, and I wanted to be there, protected by those rocks, more than anything I'd ever wanted. I knew I was being unreasonable. There was more than enough water to get by on to Wingelinna. But the camels, I'd been so sure they'd do a week comfortably. I hadn't planned on the sudden dryness—the lack of green feed. "But there'll be water there, of course there will. Haven't they told me so? What if there's not? What if the mill's run dry? What if I miss it? What if this thin little piece of string that keeps me tied to my camels breaks? What then?" Walk walk walk, sandhills for ever, they all looked the same. I walked as if on a treadmill—no progress, no change. The hill came closer so slowly. "How long is it now? A day? This is the longest day. Careful. Remember, it's just a day. Hold on, mustn't let go. Maybe a car will come. No cars. What if there's no water, what will I do? Must stop this. Must stop. Just keep walking. Just one step at a time, that's all it takes." And on and on and on went that dialogue in my head. Over and over and round and round.

Late in the afternoon—long creeping shadows. The hill was close. "Please please let me be there before night. Please don't let me be here in the dark. It will engulf me."

It must be over the next sandhill surely. No, then the next one. O.K., all right, the next, no the next, no the next. Please god, am I mad. The hill is there, I can almost touch it. I started to yell. I started to shout stupidly at the dunes. Diggity licked my hand and whined but I could not stop. I had been doing this forever. I walked in slow motion. Everything was slowing down.

And then, over the last sandhill, I was out of the dunes. I crouched on the rocks, weeping, feeling their substance with my hands. I climbed steadily, up the rocky escarpment, away from the terrible ocean of sand. The rocks were heavy and dark and strong. They rose up like an island. I crawled over this giant spine, where it emerged from the waves, in a fuzz of green. I looked back to the immensity of where I had been. Already the memory was receding—the time, the aching time of it. Already, I had forgotten most of the days. They had sunk away from memory, leaving only a few peaks that I could recall. I was safe.

Even before her trip there was a fierceness, intensity and loneliness to Robyn that both attracted and frightened people. "I was a changed woman. It seemed that anything I may have been before was a dream belonging to someone else. I was self-protective, suspicious and defensive and I was also aggressively ready to pounce on anyone who looked like they might be going to give me a hard time."

*T*HAT NIGHT, I WAS ABOUT TO TURN IN WHEN I HEARD CARS PURR IN THE DISTANCE. Aborigines. The last car, a clapped-out ancient Holden, held one young driver and three old men. They decided to stay for the night. I shared my tea and blankets. Two of the old men were quiet and smiling. I sat by them in silence, letting their strength seep in. One I especially liked. A dwarfish man with dancing hands, straight back, and on his feet, one huge Adidas and one tiny woman's shoe. He handed me the best bit of his part-cooked rabbit, dripping grease and blood, fur singed and stinking. I ate it gratefully. I remembered that I had not eaten properly for the past few days.

In the morning, I boiled the billy and started to pack up. I talked to my companions a little. They decided that one of them should accompany me to Pipalyatjara, two days' walk away, to look after me. I was so sure it was going to be the talkative one, the one who spoke English, and my heart sank. But as I was about to walk off with the camels, who should join me but—the little man. "Mr. Eddie," he said, and pointed to himself. I pointed to myself and said, "Robyn," which I suppose he thought meant "rabbit," since that is the Pitjantjara word for it. It seemed appropriate enough. And then we began to laugh.

For the next two days Eddie and I walked together, we played charades trying to communicate and fell into fits of hysteria at each other's antics. We stalked rabbits and missed, picked bush foods and generally had a good time. He was sheer pleasure to be with, exuding all those qualities typical of old Aboriginal people—strength, warmth, self-possession, wit and a kind of rootedness, a substantiality that immediately commanded respect. And I wondered as we walked along, how the word "primitive" with all its subtle and nasty connotations ever got to be associated with people like this. If, as someone has said, "to be truly civilized, is to embrace disease," then Eddie and his kind were not civilized. Because that was what was so outstanding in him: he was healthy, integrated, whole. That quality radiated from him and you would have to be a complete dolt to miss it.

However, after all that had happened to me, all that madness and strain, I desperately needed to talk in depth with someone. Because, while my panic and fear had now been supplanted by a frenetic happiness, I was still shaken to the core. I had to recover my ordinary self and make sense of the experience somehow. I was a third of the way through my trip, and Glendle, the community adviser at Pipalyatjara, would be the first and perhaps last friend I was likely to meet. I was longing to see him, to speak in English about all that had been going on. But

One night at the beginning of the trip Robyn dreamt of an old Aboriginal man who became her friend and shared the secrets of dream-time with her. Months later, just as she was beginning to feel the trip was empty and meaningless, Mr. Eddie appeared and travelled with her for the next 200 miles.

Eddie kept telling me he had "gone." I found out later that he attached the word "gone" to the ends of many sentences; it roughly implied direction so I need not have worried. But the thought of Glendle being away was too much to bear.

When Eddie walked behind I could feel him looking askance at me—feel his puzzled eyes on the back of my head. "What's wrong with this woman? Why doesn't she just relax, she keeps repeating, 'Is Glendle there, Eddie, is he there now?' "

"Glendle goooooooone," he said, waving his little hand in the air. Whenever he said that he raised his eyebrows and widened his eyes in a comical look of surprised seriousness, but I found it hard to smile. I turned and walked on, trying to control the trembling chin and the tears that threatened to bounce out of my eyeballs at any second and stream down my face.

"Please, please, you've got to be there, Glendle, I need to talk and get it all straight. I've never needed a friend like this before. Please, please be there."

We headed on to Pipalyatjara the next morning, with me feeling anxious and Eddie singing. I wasn't following maps, so I had no idea how close the settlement would be. Suddenly I noticed a tin shed on my right. I must have been staring dead ahead to have missed it. On its walls were children's drawings.

"Could that possibly be a school? Pipalyatjara doesn't have a school, does it? Glendle's the only white person here, isn't he?" I stopped and blinked. I was completely disoriented. I couldn't remember whether the drawings on the walls meant a school or not. And yet it looked like a bush school. Yes, of course, it had to be, what else. A shadow came to the door, hesitated and came strolling out rolling a cigarette. He was a rather hippieish young man, and he said in a quiet and cultivated voice, "Hello there, we've been expecting you. How's it been going?"

I gulped. I wanted to throw my arms around him, prostrate myself before him, and dance a jig. But I still didn't know how mad I was. And if I was crazy I didn't want him to realize it. So I just stared dumbly, with a great honking lop-sided grin splitting my face open and garbled, "Glendle?"

Mr. Eddie's companionship opened Robyn up to things she hadn't paid attention to before. He not only taught Robyn the names of birds and plants and the importance of places but he changed the way she experienced the passage of time.

Although Robyn began the trip eating dried food that she carried with her, as the trip progressed she began to appreciate insects and other bush foods that were relished by the Aborigines.

In addition to the occasional rabbit and shared piece of kanga-roo, Robyn tried eating witchetty grubs (top)—fat gooey worms that taste like almonds when lightly singed on a fire.

Another outback delicacy is yelka (bottom), a bush onion that may be eaten raw or cooked.

"Just turn the corner and you'll see some caravans, he's in one of those." He smiled and offered me a smoke. I was too embarrassed for him to see my shaking hands, and too afraid that I might give myself away by saying or doing something incomprehensible, so I just shook my head and walked on, wondering if he had picked anything up.

And then it struck me that people don't really mind if you're crazy out there. In fact, they half expect it and are usually slightly troppo themselves. Besides, there aren't enough people to go around for anyone to worry about whether they are dealing with a fruit-cake or not.

I knew Glendle's caravan immediately. He came out and we hugged and then hugged some more and then we hugged again and I couldn't speak so I got busy making the camels comfortable, and then we three went inside for the inevitable Australian ritual of tea-drinking. I started gibbering then, and I didn't stop raving blessed English for a minute. Or laughing.

That high lasted four days. Glendle was a most perfect, perceptive and loving host. He even gave up his crisp-sheeted bed, while he and Eddie slept outside. He swore he preferred sleeping outside and it was only laziness that prevented him from doing so more often, which was probably true. So I accepted gratefully. Not that I hadn't fallen in love with my swag by then, but experiencing the luxury of a bed again was kind of interesting.

We spent many of those nights having long heart-to-hearts. I could feel myself knitting together again, sorting it out, putting it into perspective, clearing my confusion. And I talked about Richard. I had still not rid myself of the burden of him and poor Glendle copped the lot. At the end of one particularly long and vitriolic rave, he just looked at me for a while and said, "Yes, but you're missing one important fact. Rick is a good friend to you—has done a lot for you. And anyway, it was you who invited him along, not the other way around. Can't have your cake and eat it too you know."

God knows, it was a simple enough statement of fact, but it had an effect on me. From that one conversation my obsession with Rick and Geographic, and my anger with them, began to fade.

Eddie was sticking to two things like glue. Me and my rifle. His eyesight was terrible so he could not have used it very well, but the gun never left his side. I had radioed Rick and arranged to have one the same brought out to Warburton. The old man would walk down with me to check the camels of an evening and he would carry the rifle on his shoulder and sing to himself. I felt, well, flattered

123

I suppose, that he should want to look after me in this way.

On one of these evenings we passed a group of women coming towards us. One skinny old lady in a faded dress ten sizes too big for her detached herself from the group and wandered over to about eight feet in front of us. Eddie squinted and then broke into a delighted grin. They shared a polite and obviously respectful exchange, eyes and mouths smiling at each other. I couldn't understand what was said, but I imagined that she was some old and dear friend that he'd grown up with. We walked off and he continued to smile that special happy smile to himself. I asked him who it was, and he turned to me beaming, and said, "That was Winkicha, my wife." There was such pride and pleasure in his face. I had never seen that particular quality of love shown so openly between a man and wife before. It staggered me.

That meeting between Eddie and his wife was the first insight in a series which made me realize that, contrary to what most white male anthropologists would have us believe, women hold a very strong position in Aboriginal society. While men and women have separate roles, necessitated by the enviroment, these roles are part of a single function—to survive—and both are mutually respected. With their dexterous food-gathering, the women play a greater part in feeding the tribe than do the men, whose hunting might bring in the occasional kangaroo. The women also hold their own ceremonies and play a large part in the protection of their land. These ceremonies exist parallel with the men's but it falls to the men to be the enforcers of the "law," and the caretakers of the "knowledge," made manifest in sacred objects called "tjuringas." If there is sexism amongst Aborigines today, it is because they have learnt well from the conquerors.

I remember one story, which I have never had verified, but which rings true, concerning a myth belonging to some tribe in Western Australia. In the beginning, the women had everything. They had the power to procreate, they supported the tribe and kept them alive with their knowledge of bush foods, and

Red river gum trees along the dried up Gascoyne River have massive and deep root systems that pull up to a ton of water a day from vast subterranean moisture banks. The root system is so extensive that there is more "tree" below the ground than above it.

they had a natural superiority. They also had the "knowledge" which they kept hidden in a secret cave. The men conspired to steal this knowledge, so that things would be more balanced. (Now here comes the crunch.) The women heard of this, and instead of stopping them, realized that this was the way things had to go, for the sexes to remain in harmony. They allowed men to steal this "knowledge" which has remained in their hands until today.

On the following morning, Eddie and I got ourselves ready for the walk to Warburton. Once again, all the checks and double checks and final adjustments necessary for departure had put me on overdrive, but five minutes out of the settlement, the calming rhythm of walking and the reassuring sound of the bells clanging behind, and Eddie's presence, settled me down.

We walked in silence through a hushed, lush valley. Eddie picked the plants he wanted while I watched. The vague uneasiness and fidgetiness of having the projected pattern of the day rearranged was soon soothed by the meditative way in which we searched for them. This valley was so delicate, so silent, and we didn't speak a word while we padded reverently through it. Once out of it, however, and back into the brutal afternoon sun which scorched my face, no matter how far I pulled my hat down, I again experienced that mental chafing at the bit. I tried hard to wrestle with it, push it out of my mind for good, but I was being torn by two different time concepts. I knew which one made sense, but the other one was fighting hard for survival. Structure, regimentation, orderedness. Which had absolutely nothing to do with anything. I kept thinking wryly to myself, "Christ, if this keeps up it will take us months to get there. So what? Is this a marathon or what? This is going to be the best part of your trip, having Eddie with you, so stretch it out, idiot, stretch it out. But but... what about routine...?" and so on.

The turmoil lasted all that day, but gradually faded as I relaxed into Eddie's time. He was teaching me something about flow, about choosing the right moment for everything, about enjoying the present. I let him take over.

The Gibson Desert is home to an extraordinary variety of plant and animal life; nearly ⅔ of the world's wildflowers exist only in Western Australia. The desert is also full of huge flocks of wild galahs (above)—parrots that pair for life.

Termites (right) thrive in the predominately dry conditions of the outback. In the absence of moisture-loving fungi, these insects take over the role of decomposers, consuming dead plants and releasing nutrients that replenish the desert soil.

Xanthorrhoeas or grass trees (far, upper right) was once a multiple source of food to aborigines. The flower nectar, basal leaves and shoots were eaten while the tall straight stems of the flower spikes made excellent spear shafts.

The curly bark of the Minnaritchi tree (far right) is used by the aborigines to start fires.

Known to the aborigines as Mulla-mulla, the foxtail (middle right) flowers in abundance after rain, then slowly dies back as the soil dries out.

Flora and Fauna

The country I was travelling through held my undivided attention with its diversity. This particular area had had three bumper seasons in succession and was carpeted in green and dotted with white, yellow, red, blue wildflowers. Then I would find myself in a creek-bed where tall gums and delicate acacias cast deep cool shadow. And birds. Everywhere birds. Black cockatoos, sulphur-cresteds, swallows, Major-Mitchells, willy-wagtails, quarrian, kestrels, budgerigar flocks, bronze-wings, finches. And there were kunga-berries and various solanums and mulga apples and eucalyptus manna to eat as I walked along. This searching for and picking wild food is one of the most pleasant, calming pastimes I know. Contrary to popular belief, the desert is bountiful and teeming with life in the good seasons. It is like a vast untended communal garden, the closest thing to earthly paradise I can imagine. Mind you, I wouldn't want to have to survive on bush-tucker during the drought. And even in the good season, I admit I would prefer my diet to be supplemented by the occasional tin of sardines, and a frequent cup of sweet billy tea.

I had learnt about wild foods from Aboriginal friends in Alice Springs, and from Peter Latz, an ethnobotanist whose passion was desert plant-foods. At first, I had not found it easy to remember and recognize plants after they had been pointed out to me, but eventually the scales fell from my eyes. The Solanaceae especially had me confused. These are a huge family, including such well knowns as potatoes, tomatoes, capsicums, datura and nightshades. The most interesting thing about the group is that many of them form a staple diet for Aboriginal people, while others which look almost identical are deadly poisonous. They are tricky little devils. Peter had done some tests of various species and found that one tiny berry contained more vitamin C than an orange. Since these were eaten by the thousands when Aboriginal people were free to travel through their own country, it stands to reason that their modern-day diet, almost totally devoid of vitamin C, is just one more factor contributing to their crippling health problems.

$\mathcal{A}$T NIGHT, WHEN I BUSIED MYSELF WITH UNSADDLING, EDDIE WOULD BUILD US a temporary wind-break, a wilcha. This was done expertly and quickly with a minimum expenditure of energy. I think deft is the word. He would drag old trees into a semicircle or three sides of a rectangle, clear a space of prickles for us to sleep in, and build the warming fire. No matter how many blankets I gave him, he never put these over him, but underneath. And after our meal and our talk, he would make sure I was comfortable, virtually tucking me into my swag, then he would curl up, head on his hands and fall asleep. All through the night, he would wake up, check on me and restoke the fire. He accepted the junky food I had with me but would have loved, I know, a kangaroo half-cooked in the coals. This is a delicious meat, and it is cooked by first singeing the hair and rubbing it off, then burying it in a mixture of sand and coals and leaving it for an hour. The insides are still bloody and red, but the meat and the offal sweet and juicy. There are strict rules governing the killing and cooking of kangaroo, in fact of all desert foods. Stories abounded of people who broke the law, by not killing correctly, and suffered terrible accidents because of it.

I had two knives with me, one for leather work and one for skinning and cutting up meat. Eddie asked me one day why I had two, when one would do. I explained to him that the sharp one was for game. "Marlu, kanyala," I said and mimed cutting meat. I swear the old man nearly had a heart attack. "Wiya wiya, mulapa wiya. Tsc tsc tsc tsc." He shook his head in horror. He then grabbed me by the hand and proceeded to tell me that I must never under any circumstances cut the meat of a kangaroo, or skin it, or take its tail. He repeated this over and over and I swore I would never do such a thing. And again that night, he made me promise that I would never break the law in this way. I reassured him. In any case it was extremely unlikely that I would shoot a kangaroo for myself. There was far too much meat for one person and a dog and I hated shooting these lovely animals.

Having Eddie with me was magic in terms of being accepted by Aboriginal people. Everyone knew Eddie, everyone loved him. And because he was there, and because I had camels, they loved me too. We stopped one day at a small camp by a bore—where there were maybe twenty people. We sat down together outside a humpy and talked for hours, drinking weak, cool super-sweet billy tea and chewing damper. Because I was the guest, I was given the tin mug to drink out of instead of sipping it straight from the billy like the others. The mug had been used for mixing flour and water so great clumps of the stuff floated around on top. It didn't matter. By now my attitude to food had changed utterly. Food had become something you

"The camels had a very special attitude toward children. They would let them do anything. Bub especially adored them. He would see the kids bounding towards him after school, and would immediately sit down and start to doze off in pleasant expectation of being jumped on, bounced on, pulled, tugged, pushed and walked on by the small people."

put in your mouth to give you energy to walk, that's all. I could eat anything, and did. Washing had become an unnecessary procedure by then too, I was putrid and rank and I loved it. Even Eddie, who was no sparkling example of cleanliness, suggested I should wash my face and hands one day. He was finickity about Diggity too, and refused ever to let her drink from his mug.

Neither of us liked being on the road after our time in the wild country, because we had to deal once again with that strange breed of animal, the tourist. It was very hot one afternoon, stinkingly hot, and the flies were in zillions. I had the three p.m. grumps, Eddie was humming to himself. A column of red dust hit the horizon and swirled towards us, hurtling along at tourist speed. We swerved off into the spinifex, pincushions for feet were better than idiots at this hour of the day. But they saw us, of course, a whole convoy of them, daring the great aloneness together like they were in some B-grade Western. They all piled out with their cameras. I was irritated, I just wanted to get to camp and have a cuppa and be left in peace. They plied me with questions as usual and commented rudely on my appearance, as if I were a sideshow for their amusement. And perhaps I did look a little eccentric at that stage. I had had one ear pierced in Alice Springs the year before. It had taken months to work up the courage to participate in this barbaric custom, but once the hole was made, I wasn't about to let it close over again. I had lost my stud, so I put through a large safety pin. I was filthy and my hair stuck out from my hat in sun-bleached greasy tangles and I looked like a Ralph Steadman drawing. Then they noticed Eddie. One of the men grabbed him by the arm, pushed him into position and said, "Hey, Jacky-Jacky, come and stand alonga camel, boy."

I was stunned into silence, I couldn't believe he had said that. How dare anyone be so thick as to call someone of Eddie's calibre "boy" or "Jacky-Jacky." I furiously pushed past this fool, and Eddie and I walked together away from them. His face betrayed no emotion but he agreed when I suggested that there'd be no more photos and that they could all rot in hell before we'd

Joseph and Leslie, two tribal elders,
took Robyn rabbit hunting.

talk to them. The last of the convoy arrived a few minutes later.
I reverted to my old trick of covering my face with my hat and
shouting, "No photographs." Eddie echoed me. But as I went
past I heard them all clicking away. "Bloody swine," I shouted.
I was boiling, hissing with anger. Suddenly, all five foot four
inches of Eddie turned around and strutted back to them. They
continued clicking. He stood about three inches from one of the
women's faces and put on a truly extraordinary show. He turned
himself into a perfect parody of a ravingly dangerous idiot
boong, waved his stick in the air and trilled Pitjantjara at them
and demanded three dollars and cackled insanely and hopped up
and down and had them all confused and terrified out of their
paltry wits. They'd probably been told in Perth that the blacks
were murderous savages. They backed off, handing him what
money they had in their pockets and fled. He walked demurely
over to me and then we cracked up. We slapped each other and
we held our sides and we laughed and laughed the helpless,
hysterical tear-flooded laughter of children. We rolled and
staggered with laughter. We were paralysed with it.

The thing that impressed me most was that Eddie should
have been bitter and was not. He used the incident for his
entertainment and mine. Whether he also used it for my edi-
fication I do not know. But I thought about this old man then.
And his people. Thought about how they'd been slaughtered,
almost wiped out, forced to live on settlements that were like
concentration camps, then poked, prodded, measured and taped,
had photos of their sacred business printed in heavy academic
anthropological texts, had their sacred secret objects stolen and
taken to museums, had their potency and integrity drained from
them at every opportunity, had been reviled and misunderstood
by almost every white in the country, and then finally left to rot
with their cheap booze and our diseases and their deaths, and I
looked at this marvellous old half-blind codger laughing his
socks off as if he had never experienced any of it, never been the
butt of cruel ignorant bigoted contempt, never had a worry in his
life, and I thought, O.K. old man, if you can, me too.

$\mathcal{W}$E WERE ALMOST AT WARBURTON. I HAD NOT BEEN USING MAPS AT ALL, THEY were superfluous with Eddie around. Hoping for an exact mileage, I asked some young Aboriginal people in a car how far away the settlement was.

"Hmmm, might be a little bit long way, that Warburton. Maybe one sleep, two sleeps, but little bit long way for sure."

"Oh, I see, thanks, little bit long way eh? Right. Of course."

There seemed to be several categories of distance, divided up like this: little bit way, little bit long way, long way, and long long way, too far. This last was used

Although there are thought to be over 30,000 camels running wild in Australia, the sight of Robyn and her camels attracted more than a little attention. The Aborigines, who had used camels in the 19th century, were now much more attached to mechanical forms of transportation.

for describing my distance to the sea. I would tell people I was going to the sea (uru pulka, big lake) which none of them had seen and they would raise their eyebrows, shake their heads slowly, and say, "Long, long, loooong way, too many sleeps, too far that uru pulka eh? Tsc tsc tsc." And they would shake their heads again and wish me luck, or chuckle and hold my arm and look at me, astonished.

We camped later than usual the next night. I unsaddled the camels and my heart skipped about five beats, then thumped around in my chest like a kangaroo, making up for lost time. Where was my gun? MY GUN? "EDDIE, HAVE YOU GOT MY GUN?" No gun. I had become so dependent on that rifle. In my mind's eye I pictured being sat on by a host of giant bull camels. Eddie said he'd wait while I rode back to look for it. For some unaccountable reason, I had slung the scabbard over Zeleika's saddle, and the rifle had slipped out. I headed back down the track into the delicate blue and pink glow along the eastern horizon. I rode maybe five miles, wondering when Bub would throw me to the ground and break my neck; he was shying at rocks, birds and trees, anything the imbecile could use as an excuse. I have often wondered about Bubby's neuron capacity.

A Toyota drove up. The car contained a geologist who had not only my Savage .222 over-under rifle, but Mars bars and a soft drink as well. Wonderful.

Bubby wanted to bolt back to camp. I let him pace. "O.K. you little sap, if you're so full of energy, you can carry half of Zelly's pack tomorrow." He was by far the most unreliable of the three adult camels. He had almost sent Eddie flying one day. He started to pig-root for no apparent reason and although I was leading him, he was difficult to bring back under control. Eddie clung on through it all like a monkey. I couldn't help laughing. He did not lose one iota of dignity.

I rode triumphant into camp. By this stage, I had told Eddie about the rifle that would be waiting for him in Warburton. Our conversations always ended up centred around this rifle. Was I really giving him a rifle, would it be exactly like this one, was I sure it was for him and not somebody else? Over and over he would repeat these questions, then break into a cackle when I reassured him that it was true. Every night it was the same. I also tried to tell him about Rick and *Geographic*, but what's the Pitjantjara word for American magazine? I was worried about seeing Richard in Warburton. I knew Eddie would not understand why a thousand and one photographs were really necessary. Knew he would not like it. I didn't want to jeopardize my relationship with my new friend. On the other hand, I was looking forward to seeing Rick again. And Warburton was close.

The next night was our last together on the track. Eddie insisted that he would find a reliable old man in Warburton to continue on with me to Carnegie

When it's 110° in the shade in Warburton, the dripping end of a pipe is the best place to hang out. The only danger is falling into the cattle watering hole below (which might not be so bad under the circumstances).

station. He said that it must be an old man, an elder, a wati pulka (literally "big man"), someone with a grey beard—not any young fellow. Definitely not. I was ambivalent about this. I loved being with Eddie but the next section after Warburton would be through completely wild desert, and I wanted to do that on my own—test out this new-found confidence. Four hundred miles of spinifex wastes known as the Gibson Desert, without a particle of water that I knew of. And how would that old man get back to Warburton? Eddie was O.K., Glendle was coming to pick him up. But even without that, there were enough relations travelling back and forth for him to get a lift with them. But Carnegie was a cattle station, and Warburton was the last Aboriginal outpost in that country. I decided against it. Eddie, although not pleased over this decision, accepted it.

Richard arrived in our camp at about three a.m. How he managed to find us is beyond me. He is one of those enviable people upon whom good luck falls like snow. He always managed to find me, usually through a series of unbelievable chances. His whole life runs like that. The coincidences that constantly follow him defeat statistics. He had been driving for two days, hadn't slept and was brim-full of zippy energy and enthusiasm. He had brought mail and Eddie's rifle. We chattered and laughed together, but it was plain that Eddie wanted to get back to sleep, and didn't quite know what was going on. We decided to leave the opening of presents until morning.

We all woke early. It was like Christmas morning. Eddie was ecstatic over his new rifle. I feverishly read messages from

Robyn arrived in Warburton desperately in need of a friend to talk to.

friends. Rick took photos. I had primed Eddie enough for him to expect the odd photograph. But this? Rick was sitting, kneeling, squatting, lying down, click click click click click. Eddie looked at me and scratched his head. "Who is he, what does he want, why all these photos?"

I tried to explain, but what could I say. "O.K., Rick, that's enough." Rick pulled out another camera. "Look, I've got the perfect solution." It was an S.X. 70, an instant polaroid. He took a photo of Eddie and handed it to him.

I was furious. "Oh, I see, sort of like beads for the natives. Look, Rick, he doesn't like being photographed, so quit it."

It was unfair. I knew that Rick had not meant it that way and was hurt. "The only reason I brought it," he said, "is because photographers are always promising to send photos and they never do. Besides, it's an exchange—a sharing of the image immediately." But I knew Eddie would see it as a cheap trick. And he did. He didn't like Rick, didn't like being photographed, and certainly didn't like being handed this useless bit of paper with his face on it, as a bribe. Tension.

Rick drove a couple of miles up the track and Eddie and I packed up in silence. He asked me again why this was happening and I tried again to explain. Hopeless. What I had feared might happen was happening, and out of control.

We walked up the road together. There was Rick's car with Rick standing on top, a long lens poking out of his eyeball. I decided to let Eddie handle the situation. As we approached the car, he lifted his hand, and said in English, "No photograph," then in Pitjantjara, "It makes me feel sick." I laughed. Rick captured that one moment and then desisted. When we had that photo developed much later on, there was a woman smiling at an old Aboriginal man, whose hand was raised in a cheery salute. So much for the discerning eye of the camera. That one slide speaks volumes. Or rather lies volumes. Whenever I look at it now, it sums up all the images of the journey. Brilliant images, exciting, excellent, but little to do with reality. While I love the photos Rick took, they are essentially of his trip, not my own. I don't think dear Richard has ever understood this.

Monday 11ᵗʰ July.

We went to see Robin at Snake Well. She was walking with four camels. Mr Eddie from Wingellina was with her. She started from Alice Springs and is going to Carnarvon. She has a dog named Diggetty.

Rhoda and Roelien have been camping south of here. Everyday they saw a Jumbo Jet flying overhead. (Going from Melbourne to Singapore.)

I SPENT A WEEK IN WARBURTON, FLOATING WITH HAPPINESS. I COULD NOT remember ever associating that emotion with myself before. So much of the trip had been wrong and empty and small, and so much of my life previous to it had been boring and predictable, that now when happiness welled up inside me it was as if I were flying through warm blue air. And a kind of aura of happiness was being generated. It rubbed off on people. It built up and got shared around. Yet nothing of the past five months had been anything like I had imagined. None of it had gone according to plan, none of it had lived up to my expectations. There'd been no point at which I could say, "Yes, this is what I did it for," or "Yes, this is what I wanted for myself." In fact, most of it had been simply tedious and tiring.

But strange things do happen when you trudge twenty miles a day, day after day, month after month. Things you only become totally conscious of in retrospect. For one thing I had remembered in minute and Technicolor detail everything that had ever happened in my past and all the people who belonged there. I had remembered every word of conversations I had had or overheard way, way back in my childhood and in this way I had been able to review these events with a kind of emotional detachment as if they had happened to somebody else. I was rediscovering and getting to know people who were long since dead and forgotten. I had dredged up things that I had no idea existed. People, faces, names, places, feelings, bits of knowledge, all waiting for inspection. It was a giant cleansing of all the garbage and muck that had accumulated in my brain, a gentle catharsis. And because of that, I suppose, I could now see much more clearly into my present relationships with people and with myself. And I was happy, there is simply no other word for it.

The aboriginal school children of Warburton reported on Robyn's arrival in their daybook, complete with a drawing of Mr. Eddie riding on Bub.

Robyn finally got some use out of her flying doctor radio (above) to call a friend to take Mr. Eddie home.

*From a distance spinifex scrub
appears soft but in fact the leaves
are thread-needle sharp. This
was all Robyn saw as she began the
most dangerous and lonely part
of her trek across the desolate 600
miles of the Gunbarrel Highway.*

I LEFT WARBURTON SOMEWHERE AROUND JULY. I HAD APPROXI-mately one month to go before I could expect to see another human being. Despite the fact that this leg would be the first real test of my survival skills, despite the fact that if I was going to die anywhere it would most likely be along this lonely treacherous stretch of void, I looked forward to it with new-found calm, a lack of fear, a solid reliance on myself.

Rick had decided to drive across the Gunbarrel in front of me and leave the car in Wiluna, our next meeting place. I asked him to drop a couple of drums of water for me on the way. I would need every drop of that water. The country would be dry and hot, with, presumably, little feed for the camels. Although Aboriginal people could have directed me to the rockholes, there was nothing marked on the maps. But, and I felt stupid feeling this way, I didn't want to see Rick's fresh tyre tracks all the way. I was more concerned for his safety than I was for my own. If that car broke down… I made sure he had enough water for himself, so that if that did occur, I could meet him along the track and take him with me. Glendle had also insisted that he drop two drums of water for me half way along the track. He had to drive a total of 800 wretched miles over spinifex and sand to do this—such is the quality of friends.

Throughout the trip I had been gaining an awareness and an understanding of the earth as I learnt how to depend upon it. The openness and emptiness which had at first threat-ened me were now a comfort which allowed my sense of freedom and joyful aimlessness to grow. This sense of space works deep in the Australian collective consciousness. It is frightening and most of the people huddle around the eastern seaboard where life is easy and space a graspable concept, but it produces a sense of potential and possibility nevertheless that may not exist now in any European country. It will not be long, however, before the land is conquered, fenced up and beaten into submission. But here, here it was free, unspoilt and seemingly indestructible.

And as I walked through that country, I was becoming involved with it in a most intense and yet not fully conscious way. The motions and patterns and connections of things became apparent on a gut level. I didn't just see the animal tracks, I knew them. I didn't just see the bird, I knew it in relationship to its actions and effects. My environment began to teach me about itself without my full awareness of the process. It became an animate being of which I was a part. The only way I can describe how the process occurred is to give an example: I would see a beetle's tracks in the sand. What once would have been merely a pretty visual design with few associations attached, now became a sign which produced in me instantaneous associations—the type of beetle, which direction it was going in and why, when it made the tracks, who its predators were. Having been taught some rudimentary knowledge of the pattern of things at the beginning of the trip, I now had enough to provide a structure in which I could learn to learn. A new plant would appear and I would recognize it immediately because I could perceive its association with other plants and animals in the overall pattern, its place. I would recognize and know the plant without naming it or studying it away from its environment. What was once a thing that merely existed became something that everything else acted upon and had a relationship with and vice versa. In picking up a rock I could no longer simply say, "This is a rock," I could now say, "This is part of a net," or closer, "This, which everything acts upon, acts." When this way of thinking became ordinary for me, I too became lost in the net and the boundaries of myself stretched out for ever. In the beginning I had known at some level that this could happen. It had frightened me then. I had seen it as a chaotic principle and I fought it tooth and nail. I had given myself the structures of habit and routine with which to fortify myself and these were very necessary at the time. Because if you are fragmented and uncertain it is terrifying to find the boundaries of yourself melt. Survival in a desert, then, requires that you lose this fragmentation, and fast. It is not a mystical experience, or rather, it is dangerous to attach these sorts of words to it. They are too hackneyed and prone to misinterpretation. It is something that happens, that's all. Cause and effect. In different places, survival requires different things, based on the environment. Capacity for survival may be the ability to be changed by environment.

Changing to this view of reality had been a long hard struggle against the old conditioning. Not that it was a conscious battle, rather it was being forced on me and I could either accept it or reject it. In rejecting it I had almost gone over the edge. The person inside whom I had previously relied on for survival, had, out here and in a different circumstance, become the enemy. This internal

The delicate branches of a young ghost gum glow orange in the fading desert light.

warring had almost sent me around the bend. The intellectual and critical faculties did everything they could think of to keep the boundaries there. They dredged up memory. They became obsessed with time and measurement. But they were having to take second place, because they simply were no longer necessary. The subconscious mind became much more active and important. And this in the form of dreams, feelings. A growing awareness of the character of a particular place, whether it was a good place to be with a calming influence, or whether it gave me the creeps. And this all linked up with Aboriginal reality, their vision of the world as being something they could never be separate from, which showed in their language. In Pitjantjara and, I suspect, all other Aboriginal languages, there is no word for "exist." Everything in the universe is in constant interaction with everything else. You cannot say, this is a rock. You can only say, there sits, leans, stands, falls over, lies down, a rock.

The self did not seem to be an entity living somewhere inside the skull, but a reaction between mind and stimulus. And when the stimulus was non-social, the self had a hard time defining its essence and realizing its dimensions. The self in a desert becomes more and more like the desert. It has to, to survive. It becomes limitless, with its roots more in the subconscious than the conscious—it gets stripped of non-meaningful habits and becomes more concerned with realities related to survival. But as is its nature, it desperately wants to assimilate and make sense of the information it receives, which in a desert is almost always going to be translated into the language of mysticism.

What I'm trying to say is, when you walk on, sleep on, stand on, defecate on, wallow in, get covered in, and eat the dirt around you, and when there is no one to remind you what society's rules are, and nothing to keep you linked to that society, you had better be prepared for some startling changes. And just as Aborigines seem to be in perfect rapport with themselves and their country, so the embryonic beginnings of that rapport were happening to me. I loved it.

And my fear had a different quality now too. It was direct and useful. It did not incapacitate me or interfere with my competence. It was the natural, healthy fear one needs for survival.

The moon rising through the trunk of a tree in the Gibson Desert.

*A*FTER MILE UPON COUNTLESS MILE, AFTER THE MONOTONOUS DRAG OF THOSE endless dunes, I decided that the energy required to traverse this country outweighed the pleasantness of being away from anything human. I had lost my compass, and without panic back-tracked until I found it. A stupid mistake however. Even sticking to a compass course was difficult in that country. There would suddenly rise up, in my way, a dense thicket of impenetrable bushy mulga, which, if I tried to go straight through it, caught and ripped at the pack and at me until I had to give up. This would require circling sometimes a mile out of my way. I decided to cut back on to the track. I did not know how visible the track would be. I walked thirty miles that day, hoping to find it before nightfall. It nearly killed me. My hip felt as if I had dislocated it and walking was excruciatingly painful. The limping drained away even more of my energy than the sun, which burned and seared into my face and dried and cracked my lips. The track, as it turned out, was easy to spot, and I set up camp as soon as I saw it.

At dawn I could see the Gunbarrel stretch away into the distance as far as the eye could see. And on either side of it the endless rolling spinifex plants, all delicate fronts of gold and pink which would change as the sun rose to dull grey-green horror. The seed heads made the stuff look alluring, even fragile as it bent and rippled with the cold morning breeze. How deceptive this country was. And the extremes in temperature were something to be felt to be believed. From those pale icy below-zero dawnings, to boiling midday, to the settling longed-for cool of evening and back to the crystal cold of night. I wore only trousers, light shirt and sheepskin coat which I usually took off while I was loading up. (Loading only took half an hour now.) I learnt to shiver myself warm. The other thing I learnt was not to drink during the day. I would have four or five mugs of tea in the morning, maybe a short drink at midday, and then nothing until I camped at night. It is a strange thing that, when the sun and the dry air suck gallons of sweat out of you during the day, the more you drink the more thirsty you become.

Because of the sameness of the plains, any different geographical feature was absurdly welcome. I would fall into raptures over some pitiful little gully, which could only be seen as attractive if you compared it with the country around it. One day I camped in a dust-bowl under a few straggly shadeless trees, which did more to my aesthetic senses than the Taj Mahal could do. Here would be some feed for the animals and a place where they could roll in the dirt to their hearts' content. They were unsaddled by mid-afternoon and immediately began to play. I had been watching and laughing at them for a while and suddenly, spontane-

Was this the right track or just another dead end? Along the parched Gunbarrel Highway the term "dead end" takes on new meaning. And Robyn's camels couldn't carry enough water to ensure that she would make it to the end of the 600 mile track. Glendle, Robyn's friend, drove ahead and dropped off water barrels halfway along her route. The trick was to hide the barrels and make sure that someone else didn't get to them before she did.

ously, threw off all my clothes and joined them in a romp. We rolled and we kicked and we sent the dust flying over each other. Diggity went apoplectic with delight. I was covered with thick caked orange dust and my hair was matted. It was the most honest hour of unselfconscious fun I had ever had. Most of us, I am sure, have forgotten how to play. We've made up games instead. And competition is the force which holds these games together. The desire to win, to beat someone else, has supplanted play—the doing of something just for itself.

When I left the next morning, I took out my clock, wound it, set the alarm for four o'clock and left it ticking on the stump of a tree near our dust bath. A fitting and appropriate end for that insidious little instrument, I thought, and that was that preoccupation taken care of. I executed, in celebration, clumsy little steps like a soft-shoe dancer with lead in his feet. I probably looked like a senile old derelict in fact, with my over-large sandals, filthy baggy trousers, my torn shirt, my calloused hands and feet and my dirt-smeared face. I liked myself this way, it was such a relief to be free of disguises and prettiness and attractiveness. Above all that horrible, false, debilitating attractiveness that women hide behind, "I must remember this when I get back. I must not fall into that trap again." I must let people see me as I am. Like this? Yes, why not like this. But then I realized that the rules pertaining to one set of circumstances do not necessarily pertain to another. Back there, this would just be another disguise. Back there, there was no nakedness, no one could afford it. Everyone had their social personae well fortified until they got so drunk and stupid that their nakedness was ugly. Now why was this? Why did people circle one another, consumed with either fear or envy, when all that they were fearing or envying was illusion? Why did they build psychological fortresses and barriers around themselves that would take a Ph.D. in safe-cracking to get through, which even they could not penetrate from the inside? And once again I compared European society with Aboriginal. The one so archetypally paranoid, grasping, destructive, the other so sane. I didn't want ever to leave this desert. I knew that I would forget.

Land of Ceremony

*A*s far as the Pitjantjara people were concerned they didn't own the land, the land owned them. They believed that the earth was traversed in the dream-time by ancestral beings who had supernatural energy and power. These beings were biologically different from contemporary man, some being a synthesis of man and animal, plant, or forces, such as fire or water.

The travels of these dream-time heroes formed the topography of the land, and their energies remained on earth embodied in the tracks they followed, or in special sites marking important events. Contemporary man receives part of these energies through a complex association with and duty towards these places. These are what anthropologists call totems—the identification of individuals with particular species of animals and plants and other natural phenomena. Thus particular trees, rocks and other natural objects are imbued with enormous religious significance for the people who own a particular area of country and have the knowledge of ceremonies and stories for that country.

There is no confusion in the minds of Aboriginal people as to who are the traditional caretakers of the country. Land "ownership" and responsibility is handed down through both the patriline and matriline.

The connection between dream-time, the country, and the traditional caretakers of country is manifested in the complex ceremonies that are performed by clan members. Some are increase ceremonies, ensuring the continued and plentiful existence of plants and animals and maintaining the ecological welfare of the landscape (indeed of the world); some are specifically for the initiation of young boys (making of men); and some are to promote the health and well-being of the community and so on. This detailed body of knowledge, law and wisdom handed down to the people from the dream-time is thus maintained and kept potent, and handed on through generations by the enacting of ritual.

Ceremonies are the visible link between Aboriginal people and their land. Once dispossessed of this land, ceremonial life deteriorates, people lose their strength, meaning, essence and identity.

Crossing into station country, Robyn
was appalled by the way drought
and overstocking had left a scarred
and desolate landscape. She was
worried that there would be nothing
for her camels to eat.

*A*S IF WALKING TWENTY MILES A DAY WASN'T ENOUGH, I OFTEN went out hunting or just exploring with Diggity after I had unsaddled the camels of an afternoon. On one such afternoon, I had got myself vaguely lost. Not completely lost, just a little bit, enough to make my stomach tilt, rather than turn. I could, of course, back-track, but this always took time and it was getting dark. In the past, whenever I wanted Diggity to guide me home, I simply said to her, "Go home, girl," which she thought was some kind of punishment. She would flatten those crazy ears to her head, roll her amber brown eyes at me, tuck her tail between her legs and glance over her shoulder, every part of her saying, "Why are you doing this to me. What did I do wrong?" But that evening, she made a major breakthrough.

She immediately grasped the situation; you could see a light bulb flash above her head. She barked at me, ran forward a few yards, turned back, barked, ran up and licked my hand, and then scampered forward again and so on. I pretended I didn't understand. She was beside herself with worry. She repeated these actions and I began to follow her. She was ecstatic, overjoyed. She had understood something and she was proud of it. When we made it back to camp, I hugged her and made a great fuss of her and I swear that animal laughed. And that look of pride, that unmistakable pleasure in having comprehended something, perceived the reason and necessity for it, made her wild, hysterical with delight. When she was pleased over something or someone, her tail did not go back and forward, it whipped round and round in a complete circle and her body contorted into S-bends like a snake.

I am quite sure Diggity was more than dog, or rather other than dog. In fact, I have often thought her father was a vet perhaps. She combined all the best qualities of dog and human and was a great listener. She was by now a black glossy ball of health and muscle. She must have done a hundred miles a day with her constant scampering and bounding after lizards in the spinifex. The trip, of necessity, had brought me much closer to all the animals, but my relationship with Diggity was something special. There are few humans with whom I could associate the

word love as easily as I did with that wonderful little dog. It is very hard to describe this interdependence without sounding neurotic. But I loved her, doted on her, could have eaten her with my overwhelming affection. And she never, not ever, not once, retracted her devotion no matter how churlish, mean or angry I became. Why dogs chose humans in the first place I will never understand.

O.K., you fusty old Freudians, you laudable Laingians, my psyche is up for grabs. I have admitted a weak point. Dogs.

Animal lovers, especially female ones, are often accused of being neurotic and unable to relate successfully to other human beings. How many times had friends noted my relationship to Diggity, and, with that baleful look usually associated with psychiatrists, said, "You've never thought of having a child, have you?" It's an accusation that brings an explosive response every time because it seems to me that the good lord in his infinite wisdom gave us three things to make life bearable—hope, jokes and dogs, but the greatest of these was dogs.

I was by now quite happy about camping by or on the track. The thought of anyone driving down it had long since faded into the impossible. But I had not taken into account madmen and fruit-cakes. I was awakened from my slumber one night by the roar of an engine. I struggled out of deep sleep with Diggity barking in fury, and a voice calling from the dark, "Hey, is that the camel lady, it's the overlander here. Do I have permission to enter camp?"

"What the...?"

An apparition appeared before me, with Dig biting at his trouser legs. The "overlander," as it turned out, was some nut testing a Suzuki vehicle by driving it across the widest part of Australia, over spinifex, sand and gibbers, just as fast as he possibly could. He was breaking some kind of record. He was also manic, and, presumably, out of his mind on speed. His eyeballs hung out on his cheeks and he kept slapping his upper arms, commenting on the cold, and hinting that he wouldn't mind camping here. I most certainly didn't want him camping anywhere near here, and neither did Dig. I made this quite plain without being out and out rude. He sat and raved at me for half an hour, with Dig quietly growling at the foot of my bed, and me pointedly yawning and saying very little except, "Hmm, oh really, that's nice, yawn, hmm, you don't say," and so on. He then informed me that he had been following my tracks for miles, which, considering he was coming from the opposite direction, was no mean feat. He eventually left. I scratched my head for a while, and shook it just to make sure I hadn't been hallucinating, and went back to sleep. I forgot about it. Had I known what he was going to do when he got back to civilization, I would have wrung his fat neck then and there.

On Carnegie station Robyn came across a patchwork aluminum hut used for overnight stays by station hands when out inspecting the fence lines. Some stations are over 8000 square miles and repairing fences damaged by cattle or camels is a never-ending task.

*I*ARRIVED AT CARNEGIE TO FIND IT ABANDONED AND MORE DESO-late and depressing than I can describe. Suddenly, dramatically, as soon as I hit the boundary fence, the country was ruined. Broken. Eaten out by cattle. Destroyed. I had been so in tune with the marvellous untouched country I had been through that I felt this change like a slap. How could they do this? How could they overstock their country and, with that great Australian get-rich-quick drive, lay it bare. There was nothing, not a thing, for my camels to eat. I thought I had come through the worst part, only to find the true desert, man's desert, beginning. I shouldn't be too hard on the graziers. They were suffering a four-year drought and many of their cattle had died. But there is good management and bad management, and in my opinion anyone who overstocked his country deserved everything he got. Some species of plants have disappeared from cattle country for ever, simply because of this greedy bad management. Inedible, poisonous plants (like the turpentine bush) had taken over. I had seen only very few of this species before, but now it was everywhere. It was the only green thing left alive, and it was doing very nicely thank you. Even the mulga, the only thing that would keep my camels going, was brown and dry.

I had not expected this turn of events. I had thought the going from here on would be like a holiday. I had planned to head straight through cattle country to Wiluna. I changed my

After a devastating three year drought the country west of Carnegie station was littered with carcasses, and those animals still alive were down to skin and bones. After surviving the Gunbarrel Highway Robyn had been hoping that cattle country would be more hospitable to her and the camels.

mind and studied my maps. I decided to go due north to Glenayle station, then meet up with the Canning stock route, which I thought would be free of cattle and better still, people. I had heard dreadful stories about this stock route. It had been abandoned years ago because too many cattle and camels had perished along it. It went straight through one of the worst deserts in Australia. There would be wells along it, but since these had not been kept up, most of them would be useless. However, I was only going to attempt the easiest and most southerly part and someone had told me it was glorious country. I headed off for Glenayle.

By now we all badly needed a rest. Although the country

To protect their livestock from dingoes, station owners drop strychnine-laced meat from small planes. The sight of these dead wild desert dogs strung up by station hands became increasingly common and disturbed Robyn more with each passing day.

One of the stranger sights along the way was a game of bush golf, taking place along the dirt road heading towards Wiluna.

Above right: Rumors of the "Camel Lady" started to spread and people imagined a creature which was half-woman and half-camel.

inside Glenayle was slightly better (I deduced from that, that whoever ran the place was more in tune with the land and would probably be the salt of the earth), the camels were still having a hard time getting enough to fill their bellies. My worry over them was absurd really, camels will survive where nothing else will, but Zeleika in particular was a bag of bones. Her hump had degenerated into a pitiful tuft of hair capping a set of extruding ribs. I shared out her baggage among the others, but this was not the problem. She was stupid over Goliath. He was rolling in fat and spoilt beyond redemption. The more frail she became, the more my relationship to this little parasite deteriorated. There was nothing I could do to cut down his suckling. I tried to design an udder bag but he always managed to busy his nose through it. And she would come to feed him great quantities of milk at night, no matter how close I tied him to a tree. When we stopped at midday, I always sat the camels down under some shade for an hour's rest. They deserved it, welcomed it, and would sit gazing off into the distance chewing their cuds, engrossed in deep camel speculation about the meaning of life. But I had a job keeping Goliath away from his mother. He would sneak up when I wasn't looking, nudge and push at her, demanding that she feed him. When she refused, he would grab her nose-line in his mouth and tug it. She'd bellow and leap to her feet and like lightning the little creep would dive straight at her udder. He may have been a brat but he wasn't stupid. The other nasty habit he developed was charging up beside the camels at full gallop and letting out a sideways kick at me. I put a stop to this finally by holding a large mulga waddie close to my body, then breaking it full force over his leg as he grazed perilously past—a short sharp shock that stopped him in his tracks and set him to plotting for revenge. While I grudgingly admired Zeleika's self-sacrifice, I thought she was a bit door-mattish with her first-born.

I had never chastised Diggity for chasing kangaroos, since I was certain she could never catch one. But she woke me

up that night, tearing after some poor skeletal old boomer heading out from a drink. Before I had gathered my wits to call her back, she had disappeared into the black. I went back to sleep. She returned to my swag some time later, licking me awake and whimpering, urging me to get up and follow her. "Jesus, Dig, you didn't catch it, did you?" Whimper whimper scratch lick. I loaded the rifle and followed her. She led me straight to her prize. He was a huge grey male and at death's door. I think what happened was that he was simply too weak to withstand the chase. Diggity had not touched him, wouldn't have known how to I suspect, and the poor old thing had suffered a stroke. He was lying on his side, panting softly. I knocked him on the head. The next morning, I went past the carcass and bent down with my knife to take the haunch and tail. And then I froze. What had Eddie told me about cutting meat? "But that doesn't apply to you, you're white." "Are you sure it doesn't? How do you know?" There was no way I could carry the whole kangaroo, he was much too heavy, but to leave such delicious meat just rotting there seemed crazy. After five minutes of indecision, I put the knife away and continued on.

When the beliefs of one culture are translated into the language of another culture, the word "superstition" often crops up. Perhaps it was superstition that made me leave that kangaroo intact, or perhaps it was rather that I had seen too much to be quite sure any more where truth and bogus met. Because I wasn't sure, I didn't think I was in any position to take chances.

Even with mold and fungus covering its surface this salty old cattle watering bore looked like an olympic swimming pool to Robyn.

Above right: In the outback necessity is truly the mother of invention. This enterprising galah cockatoo has taught itself to turn the water on. (The station owners are still trying to teach him how to turn it off).

*I*N A WAY, I WAS DISAPPOINTED. THE CANNING WAS TO BE THE LAST STRETCH OF NON-station country I was to see, and I thought sadly as I saddled up that the heart of the journey was coming to a close. I calculated that it would take me three weeks to reach Wiluna, the first town since Alice Springs.

The first two days were dreadful. The earth was scorched and bare, ugly grey dust covered everything and I got sick twice, the only illness I suffered on the whole trip. I had taken a freezing bore bath in the evening, and walked along naked to dry off. I woke up that night with a severe case of cystitis. Pills for that—thank the lord I brought them. But it was a sleepless night. A day or two later I found myself suffering acute stomach cramps, doubtless from some bad water I had drunk. It came on me with a sudden uncontrollable rush, and as I struggled out of my trousers, muttering ugh ugh disgusting ugh, I was overcome with—embarrassment. The desocializing process had only gone so far. I burnt the trousers, and wasted a gallon of water trying to get clean.

But after that, the country started to pick up. Whatever rains had occurred in the last four years had swept through this more northerly desert country, bypassing the cattle stations to the south. While it was anything but bountiful, there was at least a meagre picking for the beasts. What would have made me turn my nose up earlier in the trip, now appeared lush to my eyes. It was a magnificent landscape in a fossilized primordial sort of way. A twisted freakish wasteland of sandstone break-aways, silent, and seemingly aloof from the rest of the earth's evolution. God's country it may have been but it was extremely hard on the camels. The stony escarpments strained them and hurt their feet. They were carrying almost a full load of water, and I knew I would have to rest them as soon as I could find suitable water and feed.

From a study of the maps, well six looked promising. I was hot and frustrated, because I kept expecting the creekbed marked on the map to be just a little way on. It wasn't. The hill to my right was never-ending. I shouted at Diggity and laid a kick at her when she spooked the camels. I was seething with bad temper, poor little Dig had no idea what she had done wrong and walked along disconsolate with her tail between her legs. She had accepted a lot of punishment. I had a leather muzzle to put on her to protect her from strychnine baits, which were dropped way out in the desert from light aircraft to exterminate the Australian native dog, the dingo. But she had hated it. She had whined and scratched at it and looked such a picture of misery and heart-break that I eventually took it off. She was not in the habit of picking at dead carcasses and I kept her well-fed enough so that she wouldn't be tempted.

I reached the end of the hill at last, and walked down a rim of high rolling

A wild dingo casts a wary eye as Robyn passes with her entourage. "This was dingo country and I was terrified that Diggity would pick up one of the poisoned baits set out to exterminate these wild dogs."

sand-dunes. As I came over the crest, I saw an infinitely extended bowl of pastel blue haze with writhing hills and crescents floating and shimmering in it and fire-coloured dunes lapping at their feet and off in the distance some magical, violet mountains. Have you ever heard mountains roar and beckon? These did, like giant lions. A sound meant only for the ears of madmen and deaf mutes. I was paralysed by that sight. Nothing as wildly beautiful as that had I ever seen, even in my dream landscapes.

The rolling plains and plateaux covered with spinifex and blue distant mists, the vibrantly coloured sand-dunes, the deep red striated sandstone hills, and through it all, that serpentine stretch of creek-bed, all green and hard, glittering white. We skipped down that last dune and made for the well. The camels could see the feed and were straining to get there. The well itself was difficult to see and overgrown with acacia. It was fifteen feet down and smelled like rotten swamp. But it was wet and would get us by for the necessary few days. It tasted foul—like muddy soup, but with enough coffee, I could get it down.

That evening the camels played in the white dust, raising balloons of cloud that the fat, red setting sun caught, burst and turned to gold. I lay on a foot-thick mattress of fallen leaves which scattered golden jangles of firelight in a thousand directions. Night calls and leaf sighs floated down to me on the breeze and around me was a cathedral of black and silver giant ghost-gums, the thin sliver of platinum moon cradled in their branches. The heart of the world had been found. I drifted into sleep in that palace and allowed the mountains to fade along the rim of my mind. The heart of the world, paradise.

I decided to stay in that place as long as the water held out. Rick and responsibilities were so far away from me now, I didn't give them a moment's consideration. I planned to enter the sandhills and ride out to those distant mountains. But first the camels must rest. There was feed here to burn. Salt-bush, camel thorn, mulga, everything their little hearts could desire. Diggity and I explored. We found a cave in Pine Ridge which had Aboriginal paintings plastered all over it. Then we climbed a narrow, treacherous rocky gap, the wind howling and whistling

Central Australia's infamous red dust owes its powers of penetration to an incredibly fine texture. Prevailing winds have not only carried it across the continent, but traces of the dust have been found in New Zealand rain as well.

down at us. We pulled ourselves up to the flat top, where freakish rock strata ran in great buttresses and giant steps. The trees up there were gnarled into crippled shapes by the roar of the wind. Along the distant horizon I could see a sandstorm being whipped up into a cloud of red, straight out of Beau Geste. Further west, we discovered ancient desert palms, called black-boys. Rough black stumps shooting out fountains of green needles at the top, all huddled together by themselves, like an alien race left behind on a forgotten planet. There was a haunting hallucinatory quality about this place. I felt swelled by it, high as a kite. I was filled with an emotion I had not felt before—joy.

Those days were like a crystallization of all that had been good in the trip. It was as close to perfection as I could ever hope to come. I reviewed what I had learnt. I had discovered capabilities and strengths that I would not have imagined possible in those distant dream-like days before the trip. I had rediscovered people in my past and come to terms with my feelings towards them. I had learnt what love was. That love wanted the best possible for those you cared for even if that excluded yourself. That before, I had wanted to possess people without loving them, and now I could love them and wish them the best without needing them. I had understood freedom and security. The need to rattle the foundations of habit. That to be free one needs constant and unrelenting vigilance over one's weaknesses. A vigilance which requires a moral energy most of us are incapable of manufacturing. We relax back into the moulds of habit. They are secure, they bind us and keep us contained at the expense of freedom. To break the moulds, to be heedless of the seductions of security is an impossible struggle, but one of the few that count. To be free is to learn, to test yourself constantly, to gamble. It is not safe. I had learnt to use my fears as stepping stones rather than stumbling blocks, and best of all, I had learnt to laugh. I felt invincible, untouchable, I had extended myself, and I believed I could now sit back, there was nothing else the desert could teach me. And I wanted to remember all this. Wanted to remember this place and what it meant to me, and how I had arrived there. Wanted to fix it so firmly in my head

that I would never, ever forget.

In the past, my bouts of gloom and despair had led, like widdershins (water-worn gulleys), to the same place. It seemed that at that place was a signpost saying "Here it is," here is the thing you must push through, leap free of, before you can learn any more. It was as if the self brought me constantly to this place —took every opportunity to show it to me. It was as if there was a button there which I could push if I only had the courage. If I could only just remember. Ah, but we always forget. Or are too lazy. Or too frightened. Or too certain we have all the time in the world. And so back up the ravines to the comfortable places where we don't have to think too much. Where life is, after all, just "getting by" and where we survive, half asleep.

And I thought I had done it. I believed I had generated a magic for myself that had nothing to do with coincidence, believed I was part of a strange and powerful sequence of events called fate and I was beyond the need for anything or anyone. And that night I received the most profound and cruel lesson of all. That death is sudden and final and comes from nowhere. It had waited for my moment of supreme complacency and then it had struck. Late that night, Diggity took a poison bait.

We were running low on dog food, and I was too lazy, too high to want to go and shoot her some game. So I rationed her. She woke me up sneaking sheepishly back into the swag. "What's up, Dig, where've you been, little woofing?" She licked my face profusely, snuffled her way under the covers, and snuggled as usual into my belly. I cuddled her. Suddenly she slunk out again and began to vomit. My body went cold. "Oh no, no it can't be, please, Jesus, not this." She came back to me and licked my face again. "It's O.K., Dig, you're just a little bit sick. Don't worry, little one, you come and snuggle in here and get warm and you'll be O.K. in the morning." Within minutes

Termite mounds rise between clumps of spinifex.

she was out again. This couldn't be happening. She was my little dog and she couldn't be poisoned. That was impossible, couldn't happen to her. I got up to check what she had brought up. I remember trembling uncontrollably and droning to her, "It's all right, Dig, everything's all right, don't worry," over and over. She had eaten some dead animal but it didn't smell rotten, so I repeated to myself that she couldn't be poisoned. I forced myself to believe it yet I knew it wasn't true. My head raced through what you do for strychnine poisoning. You have to swing them around your head to make them get rid of it all, but even if you do it immediately there's virtually no chance of survival. "Well, I won't do that anyway, because you're not poisoned, you're not poisoned. You're my Dig and it can't happen to you." Diggity started wandering around retching violently and coming back to me for reassurance. She knew. Suddenly she ran away to some black acacia bushes and turned to face me. She barked and howled at me and I knew she must be hallucinating, knew she was dying. Her two mirror eyes burnt an image into my brain that will not fade. She came over to me and put her head between my legs. I picked her up and swung her round my head. Round and round and round. She kicked and struggled. I tried to pretend it was a game. I let her down and she went crashing through the undergrowth barking like a mad dog. I raced for the gun, I loaded it and went back. She was on her side convulsing. I blew her brains out. I knelt frozen like that for a long time then I staggered back to the swag and got in. My body shook with uncontrollable spasms. I vomited. Sweat soaked into the pillow and blankets. I thought I was dying too. I thought that when she licked me, I had swallowed some strychnine. "Is this what it feels like to die? Am I dying? No, no, it's just shock, stop it, you must go to sleep." I've never been able before or since to do what I did then. I shut my brain off and willed it into unconsciousness.

I woke well before dawn. The sick, steely, pre-dawn light was enough to find the things I needed. I caught the camels and gave them some water. I packed my belongings and loaded up. I felt nothing. Then suddenly it was time to leave that place and I didn't know what to do. I had a profound desire to bury the dog. I told myself it was ridiculous. It was natural and correct for the body to decay on the surface of the ground. But there was an overwhelming need in me to ritualize, to make real and tangible what had happened. I walked back to Diggity's body, stared at it, and tried to make all of myself face what was there. I didn't bury her. But I said goodbye to a creature I had loved unconditionally, without question. I said my goodbyes and my thank-yous and I wept for the first time and covered the body with a handful of fallen leaves. I walked out into the morning and felt nothing. I was numb, empty. All I knew was I mustn't stop walking.

Throughout the trip, whenever the camels were nervous or edgy, they would seek Robyn's company. With Diggity gone Robyn turned to her camels for comfort.

179

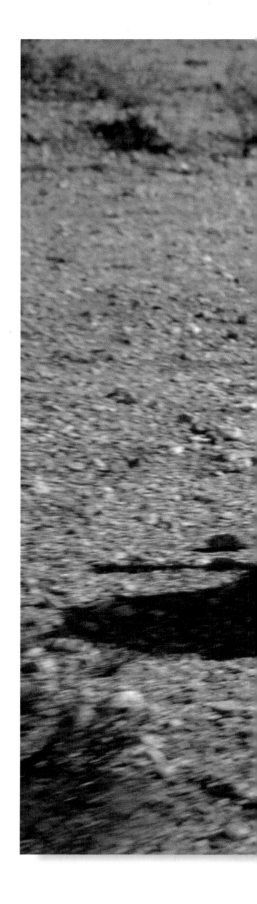

I MUST HAVE WALKED THIRTY OR MORE MILES THAT DAY. I WAS AFRAID TO STOP. AFRAID that the feeling of loss, guilt and loneliness would swamp me. I pulled into a wash-away and built a bonfire. I had hoped to be so exhausted that I would fall asleep without having to think. I was in a strange state. I had been expecting a lack of control over my emotions, but instead I was cool, rational, hard-edged, accepting. I decided to finish the trip in Wiluna, not because I was wanting to run away from it, but because I felt that the trip had ended itself; had reached some psychological conclusion, had simply become complete, like the last page of a novel. I dreamt that night, and most following nights for months, that Diggity was all right. In my dreams I would relive the sequence of events, only it always turned out that she survived, and that she forgave me. She was often human in these dreams, and talked to me. They were disturbingly vivid. I woke to the reality of loneliness, and was surprised at the strength which enabled me to accept it.

It may seem strange that the mere death of a dog could have such a profound effect on someone, but, because of my isolation, Diggity had become a cherished friend rather than simply a pet. I'm sure, had the incident occurred back in the city, surrounded by my own kind, the effect would not have been anywhere near as great. But out there, and in that changed and stretched state of mind, it was as traumatic as the death of a human, because to a large extent she had become just that, she had taken the place of people.

I was woken that night by the most chilling, hair-lifting sound I had ever heard. A soft, high-pitched keening that got louder and louder. I had never been afraid in the dark, and if I heard a sound I couldn't place, it didn't disturb me too much. Besides, Dig had always been there to protect and comfort me. But this? Ripples ran up and down my back. I got up and wandered around camp. Everything was perfectly still, but the noise was now a continuous unmodulated wail. I began to recognize the first tell-tale signs of panic–this noise had to have a rational explanation. Either that, or I was going mad, or some spirit was out to drive me that way. Then I felt the first stirrings of breeze. Of course, the noise I was hearing was the wind whistling through the top tips of the trees. There had not been a breath of turbulence on the ground, but now the pre-dawn wind, that solid unflagging front of cool air, was chilling me to the bone and making the coals of the fire glow red. I crawled back into my swag shivering, and tried to get back to sleep. I would have given anything just then, to be able to hold that familiar warm dog flesh–the need was like a physical ache. Without her, I was suddenly susceptible to all those swamping, irrational feelings of vulnerability and dread.

Most of the rest of that week or ten days was a timeless blur. The ground

Robyn's favorite outback animal was the ostrich-like emu, a inquisitive creature. She would often look up from her campfire and see dozens of curious eyes staring back at her from the darkness. When frightened, instead of sticking their heads in the ground, emus run away at a remarkable 30 miles per hour—and they have good reason to run. Aborigines hunt their delicate flesh and huge green eggs.

travelled under my feet unnoticed until some piece of country shocked me out of my mental machinations. I kept getting the odd sensation that I was in fact perfectly stationary, and that I was pushing the world around under my feet.

At about this time I entered and spent a day exploring what was probably the most impressive surreal piece of landscaping I had seen on the whole journey. A vast depression had sunk away from a broken plateau. Rimming it all around the horizon were cliffs of every imaginable hue. Some of these faces were as smooth and glossy as fine porcelain. Some were pure dazzling white, some pink, green, mauve, brown, red and so on. The depression was covered in samphire, which I then thought was "sand-fire." It was such a perfect name. When this plant dried out, it changed into myriads of colours—rainbow colours, reflecting the flow and iridescence of the cliffs. And dotted throughout this lost world were weirdly sculptured mounds of rock and pebbles. A martian landscape seen through multi-coloured glasses. I picked up and kept one small rock—pale pink sandstone studded with glitter, one side rippled into tiny sharp ridges.

The other topographic freaks that stopped me in my tracks were the claypans. Mile after mile these perfectly flat brown hard-baked Euclidean surfaces ran, without a blade of grass on them, without a tree or an animal or a clump of spinifex—nothing but towering, thin, crooked, brown pillars of whirling dust being sucked up into a burning, almost white sky. Looking at these claypans was like gazing at a calm ocean, only you could walk on this stuff. Right next to one huge pan was a dwarf replica, about a hundred yards across. A bush ballroom. An outback amphitheatre. I tied up the camels for their midday break and in that searing, clean, bright, dry heat, I took off my clothes and danced. I danced until I could dance no more—I danced out everything, Diggity, the trip, Rick, the article, the whole lot. I shouted and howled and wept and I leapt and contorted my body until it refused to respond any more. I crawled back to the camels, covered in grime and sweat, shaking with fatigue, dust in my ears and nose and mouth, and slept for about an hour. When I woke, I felt healed, and weightless, and prepared for anything.

I was well and truly back in station country now. The tracks here were well used. I had a bath and a swim at the next bore, washed my hair and clothes and hung them on the saddle to dry. And I promised myself as I walked along that I would eat properly that night—I was too light-headed, too close to the edge to continue on the way I was doing, and I needed to bring myself down.

I spotted a vehicle coming. I thought it must be station people out to do their check on the bores. It wasn't bush folk. It was the jackals, hyenas, parasites and pariahs of the press. By the time I saw the long-lens camera trained at me, it was too

After days of endless flat horizons Robyn suddenly came across this rock formation at Pine Ridge. The Ridge is located along the Canning Stock Route, a former cattle trail across the bleak stretch which runs from Halls Creek to Wiluna.

late to hide, or get out the gun and blast it at them, or even realize that I was crazy enough to do such a thing. Out they spilled.

"We'll give you a thousand dollars for the story."

"Go away. Leave me alone. I'm not interested."

My heart was pumping like a cornered rabbit's.

"Well, for Christ's sake, might as well come and have a cold beer anyway."

They had the human psyche so well tapped that they could bribe me with one beer where they couldn't buy me for a thousand bucks. I accepted the bribe as much to find out what was happening back in the world, and why they were here, as anything else. They sneaked in a few questions.

"Where's your dog?"

I didn't know how to sidestep these people—had once again forgotten the rules of the game.

"She's dead, but please don't print that as it would make a few old people back home very distressed."

"Yeah, O.K., we won't."

"Is that a promise—your word?"

"Sure, sure."

But they did print it of course. They flew back to Perth with a scoop, made up a story, and the myth of the romantic, mysterious camel lady was launched.

When the first wave of press descended on Robyn near Wiluna, she felt invaded and, even more, dismayed to find that she was on the front page of newspapers around the world. Newspapers, magazines and TV networks had sent teams of reporters to track down "The Mysterious Camel Lady."

With each passing day more stories about the "Camel Lady" appeared in the media. More reporters, eager for a firsthand story, poured into Wiluna. Robyn considered abandoning her trip for fear that reporters would follow her every step the rest of the way.

THAT NIGHT I CAMPED WELL OFF THE ROAD IN A DENSE THICKET. THIS WAS something I had not expected at all. Those light planes I had seen buzzing around all day and vaguely felt curious about were for me. What on earth had got into those people back there? I had noticed a kind of hysteria in the reporters when they talked of the press reports. "Worldwide," they had said. I couldn't believe that. I decided to wait there for a couple of days. If the press were really after me it would be better to hide out until it all blew over.

It was the overlander who had really set me up. When he arrived back in civilization, longing for any limelight he could stand under, he told a story of this marvellous woman he had "spent a night with" in the desert. The quote ran something like, "It was romantic. Her bare shoulders protruded from the sleeping bag, bells were tinkling on the pack, and I talked with her for many hours in the moonlight. I didn't ask her why she was doing it, she didn't ask me why I was doing it. We understood." Not a bad description of a sun-crazed loony in a sweat-soaked, camel-bespattered, grimy swag, who had been innocently pushing up zeds from the pit at the time. The worm.

I ran into the bushes when the first cars arrived, television cameras and all. These jerks had hired a black tracker. But my fighting spirit was coming back to me now. They were so stupid, so heavy, these people—they didn't belong here and I had the edge on them there at least. I giggled to myself and whispered silent Indian war whoops from behind my camouflage. I circled right round through the thicket so that I was only twenty feet from them. The place where I had camped was sandy, so a blind fool could have tracked me. My footprints stood out like neon signposts, like Mac truck tracks on a sandhill.

"All right, fella, where is she?" One of them, the fat one with sweat staining his red T-shirt and a scowling heat-struck look over his matching face, addressed the black tracker.

"Gee, boss, that camel lady might be real smart one, she might be cover up them tracks. I can't see where she gone." And he shook his head and rubbed his chin in thoughtful puzzlement.

Yippee and whoop whoop. I could have leapt out and kissed him for that. He knew exactly where I was and he was on my side. The fat one cursed and grudgingly handed over the ten dollars' wages. The Aborigine smiled and put it in his pocket, and they took off—150 miles of dirt track back to Wiluna.

I went back to my camp, stoked up the fire and felt raw. Invaded. As if my skin had been pulled off. I felt vulnerable and my stomach had knotted into

MYSTERY GIRL ROBIN CROSSES 'KILLER' DESERT BY CAMEL

Over the hump—into a legend

ABOUT the only things that survive in the [wil]d Australian [wil]derness called [Gib]son Desert — [nam]ed after one of its [vict]ims—are legends.

[The]re's one about ['Las]seter's Reef," a [moun]tain of gold found, [but] never rediscovered. [Ex]plorer H. B. Lasseter [in] the desert claimed [mor]e than half a cen[tury] ago.

[An]other concerns the [myst]erious death there of [Le]drich Leichardt, [Austra]lia's greatest ex[plorer] who disappeared [atte]mpting an east-west [cross]ing of the continent in 1848.

[No]w another legend is in [the] making.

[The] Camel Lady of [Neve]r-Never Land as [loc]es call the area, [rath]er than the British [term] where no rain has [fal]len within living [mem]ory and where the [gro]und is so hard that [hea]vy vehicles leave no [m]aking.

[To a]ll good legends the [tale] of 27-year-old Robyn [David]son's epic journey [add]ed the outside world [anoth]er tantalising frag[ment]. . . .

AMAZED

[A] half-believed report [of] an outback rancher [who] radioed to anyone [list]ening that he had seen ["a] beautiful, beautiful [gir]l lady," came first.

[A] police report followed [of] then a traveller on [the] edge of the Gibson— [an] area mined for [min]rela riches old [cen]ter predicted were [als]o — brought in a [blurr]ed photograph.

[Fin]ally a report to the [Flyin]g Doctor base at [Me]kathara came in about [the] mysterious lady.

[The] radio operator there, [Ian] Catchpole who emi[grated] from Ipswich seven [year]s ago, reported : . . . [Ever]yone is amazed [tha]t this girl should be [atte]mpting such a journey. [In] the old days farmers [dro]ve their cattle [throu]gh the desert to mar[ket i]n Wiluna. It took [thre]e or four months and [man]y didn't all make it.

[N]obody knows much [abou]t Miss Davidson. She [is k]eeping her movements [very] quiet and is delibers[ate]ly avoiding publicity."

At the tiny township of Wiluna on the Western edge of the Gibson Desert, locals are waiting for Robyn's arrival.

The last report was from a ranch 150 miles away. Said Wiluna policeman Robert Priddis: "She told the people at the ranch she was English, but that was all.

"Planes have already been up looking for her, but in that wilderness it is almost impossible. Even if they did locate her they wouldn't be able to land."

Last night a few more facts came to light.

Robyn, apparently raised in the harsh Australian outback near Alice Springs, had long dreamed of crossing the dead regions "to have one of life's great adventures and to see something of our native aboriginal culture

DANGER

"I'm relying on bush tucker," she wrote, "and I must say I don't like it very much."

She was shooting kangaroo before entering the desert and living on fat white widgery grubs which friendly aboriginals helped her to find.

She also has thanks for the aborigines who helped her find her way across the trackless wastes. "They have a kind of emotional map in their heads," she reported.

The only danger she spoke of came from wild bull camels, apparently an ever present threat to female camels.

Forewarned by Alice Springs camel breeder Noel Fullerton, however, she is forearmed with a shotgun-cum-rifle.

In one of her messages to the magazine Robyn wrote: "I'm looking forward to a hot bath and an iced drink when I do get through to Wiluna. But I wouldn't have missed any of this."

Latest report of Robyn came from the magazine last night. "She has sent us word that she is over the worst of the journey—and is enjoying it."

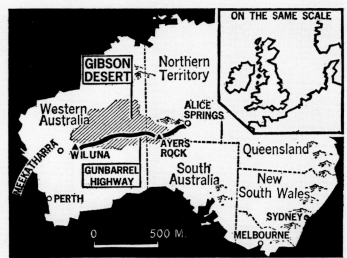

ON THE SAME SCALE

GIBSON DESERT · Northern Territory · Western Australia · ALICE SPRINGS · MEEKATHARRA · WILUNA · AYERS ROCK · GUNBARREL HIGHWAY · South Australia · Queensland · New South Wales · PERTH · SYDNEY · MELBOURNE · 0 — 500 M.

Robyn's route across Australia's killer wastelands

> **'The worst of the journey is done . . . now I'm looking forward to a hot bath and an iced drink'**

The mystery of the English Camel Girl should be solved in about a week.

Amazing journey

By FRANK CROOK

For Robin Davidson, 28, who is crossing the Gibson Desert by camel, is only 80km from the small West Australian township of Wiluna.

And when she arrives there she may tell why she is making the trip — accompanied by four camels and a dog — through some [of Aus]tralia's most in[hospitable] country.

So far she h[as spoken] to only a na[rrow range of] people about [the journey] which began [at Alice] Springs two mon[ths ago.]

She has met [with station] owners along [the way] and also chatt[ed during] a midnight can[p with a] marathon car-c[rew.]

The driver, I[an Bartell can] tell, told how h[e met Miss] Davidson du[ring his] record-breaking [crossing] of the desert.

'Roman[ce'?]

"As two adv[enturers I] felt we had sor[nething in] common," he s[aid.]

"To me she w[as beauti]ful.

"It was very [still] with the tink[le of the] camel bells."

Bartell said [Miss Da]vidson's only c[oncern] for the word, [and] "she just wan[ted to do] it."

Miss David[son has] covered m[ore than] 1300km since [she left] Alice Springs.

But after cr[ossing the] desert she fac[es a jour]ney of almost [800km to] Carnarvon, on [the West] Australian coas[t.]

Miss Davidso[n has al]ready passed [into] folklore becau[se of her] epic journey a[s one of] the first woma[n to cross] the Gibson [Desert by] camel.

Senior Cons[table Ro]bert Priddis, [in] charge of the [Wiluna] police station [has] said today h[e expected] the Camel Lad[y within] a week.

"It's pretty [rough] out there," he [said.]

worst part of her trip will be over.

"It's still a long haul to Carnarvon, but the

Constable P[riddis . . .]

he had no plans to meet up with the Camel Lady

Camel lady looked great by moonlight

By PAUL HEINRICHS

There's movement at Wiluna, 940 kilometres north-east of Perth — for the word has got around that the Camel Lady of the Gibson Desert is coming to town.

The mysterious Camel Lady, reported to be about 25 and beautiful under desert moonlight, has humped her bluey nearly 1000 kilometres west from Ayers Rock with four camels and a dog.

No one in inland Western Australia quite knows who she is, where she comes from or why she's doing it — but that hasn't stopped them speculating.

But in Melbourne yesterday, an Adelaide adventurer who spent "a glorious hour and a bit" with the Camel Lady by a campfire in the desert wasn't giving much away.

"I said to her that I wasn't going to ask why she was doing it — we both knew why we were doing what we were," said Dennis Bartell, Adelaide farmer and company director.

Yesterday's latest came from Constable Mick Leverence, of Wiluna, who said she was now only about 250 kilometres north-east of the town.

Constable Leverence said she arrived at Henry Ward's million-acre Glenayle station "a short while ago" — by which he meant a week or so.

By now, he reckoned, the Camel Lady would be pretty near Well 10 on the Canning stock route, and about to to turn south towards Wiluna.

The track goes under the misnomer of the Gunbarrel Highway — which Constable Leverence says is "a hell of a rough track". Its landmarks are the Giles Weather Station near the WA-South Australian border and Carnegie Station— separated by hundreds of kilometres.

By radio telephone from Ayers Rock, one of the ranger staff, Mr. Peter Fannin, said the Camel Lady was there "some couple of months ago.

"The last report that I heard was that she had trouble with wild camels. She had to shoot two wild bulls who were attracted by her females," he said.

Mr. Bartell, 44, smelt the Camel Lady's campfire smoke and stopped while on the west-east section of what is believed to be the first lone vehicle two-way crossing of Australia at its widest point.

"When I saw the fire, I jammed on the brakes and called out 'I'm the Overlander, is that the Camel Lady?'. A little voice came back saying 'yes'. So I called out again 'The Overlander requests permission to enter camps.'

"She was beautiful. The moon was out, the camel pack was standing at the edge of the mulga with their bells tinkling.

"I remember I was freezing, and I was huddling round the fire. She was in her swag, and she could have been as ugly as ugly, but she was a beautiful thing for me."

a tight cold ball of tension. What in god's name was happening here? People had done trips like this before, how come I was copping the attention? I still had no idea of the extent of the furore. I thought of covering my tracks but that wouldn't fool any Aboriginal—eventually one of them would find me. I thought of scaring them all off with a few shotgun pellets but dropped that immediately—it would just be another story.

And then I saw Rick's car charging past at the speed of light with several other cars chasing him. "Oh my god, what IS going on?" Rick came back in five minutes, turned in on my tracks and drove up to me. He only just had time to give me a vague outline before they all piled out. Some were from the London press, some were from television, some were from the Australian papers. I hissed and snarled and ground my teeth at them. I stomped into the bushes and ordered them point-blank from behind a tree to put their cameras down. Rick told me later that I looked and behaved like a mad woman. Exactly what they had expected. I had washed my hair in a salty bore, so it stuck out of my head in a frizzed, bleached electric halo. I was frazzled and burnt black by the sun and I hadn't been sleeping much in the last week or so, so that my eyes were piggy little slits, with brown sag beneath them. I was also out of my tree. I had not recovered from the loss of Diggity and couldn't handle this invasion of what looked to me then like inter-galactic war-lords. I was so adamant and so crazy that they shuffled their feet with embarrassment and did as they were told. I came back. And then, like a fool, I partially relented. When I look back I marvel at myself. At what makes me instantly apologetic to people I have stood up to when they have been prepared to walk all over me. I still allowed no photos so one of them photographed my campfire. "Can't go back with nothing, I'd get fired."

Others rationalized my dislike for publicity by saying, and later printing, that I was committed to a magazine, that I had done the trip for the magazine and therefore couldn't talk to anyone else about it. Why couldn't they understand that some of us just don't want to be famous—that anonymity cannot be bought for any price, once you have lost it? They left eventually, and Rick and I were free to talk. He told me of his own ordeal. Of reading in some obscure overseas newspaper of how the camel lady was lost, and how he had not slept for four days trying to reach me before the wave of reporters did, and wondering if

I were dead. He had been leapt upon by reporters in Wiluna and had tried, unsuccessfully, to shake them off. He showed me some of the papers he had picked up. Pictures of me smiling into the camera.

"How the hell did they get hold of these?" I was stunned.

"Tourists have been selling them to the papers."

"JeeeeeeSUS."

Some of the reports were at least entertaining. They said things like, "Miss Davidson lived on berries and bananas [?] and said she would kill her camels for meat if she was starving," or, "Miss Davidson was met by a lone and mysterious Aboriginal man one night who travelled with her for a time, then disappeared, as silently as he had come," or (this from an American bush-walker's magazine), "No points this week to Robyn Davidson the camel lady, for wilfully destroying the Australian native [?] camel. Perhaps she thought she was on a big game hunt." Idiots.

And enemies had suddenly switched sides. All those people back in Alice Springs who wouldn't have spat on me if I were burning in those frugal, anonymous days, were suddenly on the publicity bandwagon. "Sure," they said, "I knew her. I taught her everything she knows about camels."

And it was only then that I realized what I had let myself in for, and only then I realized how bloody thick I had been not to have predicted it. It would seem that the combination of elements—woman, desert, camels, aloneness—hit some soft spot in this era's passionless, heartless, aching psyche. It fired the imaginations of people who see themselves as alienated, powerless, unable to do anything about a world gone mad. And wouldn't it be my luck to pick just this combination. I was now public property. I was now a feminist symbol. I was now an object of ridicule for small-minded sexists, and I was a crazy, irresponsible adventurer (though not as crazy as I would have been had I failed). But worse than all that, I was now a mythical being who had done something courageous and outside the possibilities that ordinary people could hope for. And that was the antithesis of what I wanted to share. That anyone could do anything. If I could bumble my way across a desert, then anyone could do anything. And that was true

The camels were oblivious to all of this attention but they sensed that Robyn was unhappy. Bub, the clown, ostensibly came to give Robyn a cuddle but the moment she let her guard down, he tried to steal some of her food.

especially for women, who have used cowardice for so long to protect themselves that it had become a habit.

The world is a dangerous place for little girls. Besides, little girls are more fragile, more delicate, more brittle than little boys. "Watch out, be careful, watch." "Don't climb trees, don't dirty your dress, don't accept lifts from strange men. Listen but don't learn, you won't need it." And so the snail's antennae grow, watching for this, looking for that, the underneath of things. The threat. And so she wastes so much of her energy, seeking to break those circuits, to push up the millions of tiny thumbs that have tried to quelch energy and creativity and strength and self-confidence; that have so effectively caused her to build fences against possibility, daring; that have so effectively kept her imprisoned inside her notions of self-worthlessness.

And now a myth was being created where I would appear different, exceptional. Because society needed it to be so. Because if people started living out their fantasies, and refusing to accept the fruitless boredom that is offered them as normality, they would become hard to control. And that term "camel LADY." Had I been a man, I'd be lucky to get a mention in the Wiluna Times, let alone international press coverage. Neither could I imagine them coining the phrase "camel gentleman." "Camel lady" had that nice patronizing belittling ring to it.

Robyn temporarily managed to lose the press and found some momentary peace in the desert solitude.

Many of the local people were sympathetic to Robyn's desire to be left in peace. A talented local tracker named Peter Muir, his wife Dolly and their son befriended Robyn. They offered to hide her and the camels on their homestead until the press ran out of patience and expense accounts.

RICK HAD MET A MAN IN TOWN—PETER MUIR. AN EX-DOG-ger, brilliant tracker, and who turned out to be one of the finest, multi-talented bushmen I have ever met—a dying breed. Peter and Dolly came out to visit and told us what was happening in Wiluna. The town was being invaded by reporters offering money to anyone who could find me—a kind of siege; the police were receiving international calls all through the night, and were, understandably, ready to wring my neck; and the flying doctor radio was clogged with calls, to the point where real emergencies were not getting through. I was really angry now—deep down seething angry. Oddly enough, all the people in Wiluna were on my side. As soon as they heard that I didn't want the publicity they went out of their way to protect me from it. The town clammed up.

Peter and Dolly offered me their second house, several miles out of Wiluna, to hide in. The people at Cunyu invited me to let my camels stay in their horse paddock, and continued to play dumb as to my whereabouts.

"Camel lady? Sorry, mate, no idea."

I drove into Wiluna with Rick and then he told me that he had arranged for Jenny and Toly to come out and see me. Dear Rick. They were just what I needed.

After stocking up our hideaway with luxuries, we drove to Meekatharra, a slightly larger town a hundred miles west, to pick up Jen and Toly from the airport. I couldn't speak when I first saw them, but I held on to them tight. Seeing them and touching them was like a dose of tonic. They understood. They stroked my ruffled feathers and forced me to laugh at the insanity of it all. I began to feel less like a hunted criminal and more like a normal human being. Friendship in certain subsections within Australia amounts almost to religion. This closeness and sharing is not describable to any other cultural group to whom friendship means dinner parties where one discusses wittily work and career, or gatherings of "interesting" people who are all suspicious, wary, and terrified of not being interesting after all.

We laughed and joked and shed a few tears that day, and went to play pool in the local pub, where a woman (the local runner for the A.B.C.) noticed Rick's cameras and asked him if he knew where the camel lady was. He answered that he'd heard she was going to be in Meekatharra in about a week's time, and from there was travelling south, but could she please not print that as he knew the camel lady was extremely upset over the publicity. She tsc tsced, and said yes, wasn't it awful, poor thing, etc., and immediately skulked home to type out a piece which put everyone off the scent and had us rolling in the aisles. Rick had said all that with a perfectly straight innocent face, and begged her in the name of common decency to do the right thing, knowing full well that she would not.

We left Wiluna a few days later. My last night with Jen and Toly on the track finally convinced them that camels are virtually human. Mine had a habit of hanging around camp, looking for hand-outs, or waiting until I wasn't watching so they could sneak their long-lipped faces into the food bags. As we ate dinner that night, we were entertained by Dookie, who kept trying to get at the large tin of honey he knew was hidden in a pack-bag just near where I was sitting. I told him to piss off. There followed a game of, "See how far you can push Rob without getting a clout." He inched forward ever so nonchalantly. Had he been human the parallel behaviour would have been hands behind back, eyes gazing up at the sky, and whistling. We pretended to keep eating but we were all watching him out of the corner of our eyes. He made a dive for the bag, I flicked him on the lips and he retreated about six inches. We continued eating. And then, to Toly's uncontrollable hysteria, Dookie pretended to eat a completely dead bush, his eyes rolling so he could keep his beady stare on the honey, and when he thought he had fooled us sufficiently with his innocence and diversionary tactic, he

Robyn's friends Jenny and Toly flew out to meet her. For a week all thoughts of the trip were put aside.

It was a relief to have people there that she could trust and with whom she could talk freely.

dived for the bag and tried to take off with it. "All right, Rob, I take it back, you don't anthropomorphize at all."

Those next couple of weeks with Rick were easy and pleasant. The strange thing about being with a person in a desert is that you either end up the bitterest of enemies or the closest of friends. It had been touch and go in the beginning. Now, without the pressure of my feeling he had robbed me of something, or rather, with my acceptance of things turning out the way they did, plus the fact that Rick was a changed person, the friendship was firmly cemented. It had a rock-hard basis called shared experience, or the tolerance developed from seeing someone at their best and at their worst, and stripped of all social value—the bare bones of another human being. He had learnt a great deal from that trip; sometimes I think he got far more out of it than I did. We had shared something miraculous which had fundamentally changed us both. We knew each other very well I think. Besides, he had now moved out from behind his camera and become part of the trip.

He had been extremely upset over the death of the dog. I don't think he had ever had a pet and this was the closest relationship to an animal he'd experienced. They had been nauseatingly in love with one another. I had never seen Diggity take to a person like that before. A couple of weeks out from Wiluna, Rick returned to camp late one night, after having driven a few hundred wretched miles of mercy run to pick up feed—he was extremely tired and he was not feeling well. He woke me up from a particularly disturbing dream in which Diggity was circling camp, whining, but would not come when I called her. Rick was quite out of it with exhaustion, and when he came over to me he said, "Hey, what's Diggity doing over there—I nearly ran over her when I came into camp." He had forgotten. I don't know how to explain that one—won't even try to, but it was not the only incident of its kind that happened in those weeks.

a crow on jam tins really. Yeah, nothing but crow-bait, poor old cow." Zeleika, who looked now like an Auschwitz survivor, was standing with the other two healthy bullocks. The man calmly walked up to Dookie, looked at him thoughtfully, shook his head slowly and sadly and said, "Yeah, by crikey, you've got yourself a sick camel there all right. Poor old blighter. Tsc tsc tsc. Dunno what you can do for her though." Richard and I tried gallantly to control our sputtering and smirking, while the man continued to tell us about camels. Richard drove him back to the plane, he took off in a cloud of bull-dust, dipped his wings and flew home. We still laugh over that.

A day later, we clanged into Dalgety. After a week there, Zeleika had improved to the extent that I thought she would easily make it to the coast. I believed a swim would do the old girl a power of good. I had kept Goliath away from her with the aid of cattle yards and this had sped her along the road to recovery. The calf did not stop screaming and wailing and cursing me for one second, even though I gave him bucket after bucket of milk and molasses. Little pig. It was traumatic for Zeleika too—she kept trying to press her udder through the railing for him to suckle. Another week of pampering and she looked better than she had for the whole trip. She even managed a buck or two in the early morning light.

I decided to take them all to Woodleigh station, where Jan and David Thomson were eagerly awaiting our arrival. The property was a mere fifty miles from the ocean, and a blessed one hundred miles from Carnarvon, the welcoming committee and the press. I was still nervous about reporters, so just to make sure they wouldn't hunt me down, we decided to send a fake telegram from me to Rick,

Injecting Zelly with terramycin (left). While Robyn nursed Zelly she reciprocated with an affectionate nuzzle (right).

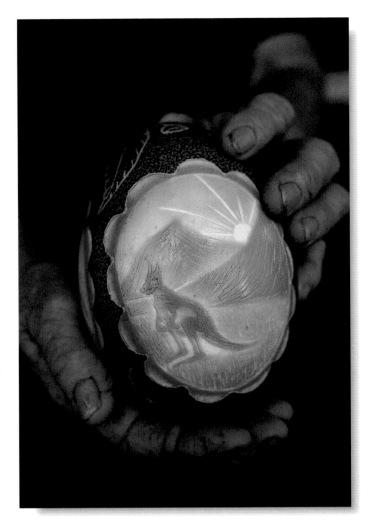

saying "Zeleika still ill, will be in Carnarvon mid-November"—a dirty trick, but a good one as I discovered later on. I wanted to travel this last short distance by myself and Rick and I arranged to meet at Woodleigh in a few weeks' time.

The weather was turning now. There is no real spring or autumn in the desert. The weather is either cold, hot, very hot, or bloody hot. It was getting into the bloody hot. While the stations around Dalgety consisted of good fertile country, red ridges of sand covered in stunted khaki-coloured scrubby trees called wanyu—a kind of mulga that was meant to be reasonable camel fodder, but which mine refused to touch. They had never seen it before. Within days they lost all the condition they had built up at Dalgety. I tried to convince them it was delicious but they didn't believe me. Didn't trust me. And there was virtually nothing but wanyu. By the time I reached Callytharra, the last station before Woodleigh, I was again worried about them.

I was only a couple of days from Woodleigh now, and of course everything started to disintegrate. The pack suddenly developed holes and rips, saddles began rubbing camel backs overnight, and my last pair of trusty sandals broke. I had to tie them on with string, which hurt and cut into my feet, because I could not go barefooted any longer. You could have fried an egg on that sand. And the country was all the same, the bores were salty and warm and I just wanted

"These two people astonished me. They had nothing. No electricity, no money, and the drought had hit them badly. And somehow they clung on, remained kind, generous, warm and uncomplaining. Of all the outback people I met on the trip, I think George and Lorna personified battling bush spirit the best. They were extraordinary people. They shared with me everything they had."

Lorna's hobby was carving extraordinarily delicate and intricate tableaux on the fragile surface of emu eggs (above right).

The last challenge of Robyn's trip was to find a good home for the camels once they had reached the ocean. "I decided to take them all to Woodleigh station, a mere fifty miles from the ocean. It's hard to say who Jan and David Thomson were more pleased to see—me or the camels. I knew my beasts could enjoy a happy and pampered retirement here."

to get to Woodleigh and sit in some shade and drink cups of tea. I had taken my clothes off because of the heat when I stumbled across the homestead. It was marked wrongly on the map and I came upon it ten miles too soon. I hastily dressed and clanged up to the house. It's hard to say who Jan and David were more pleased to see — me or the camels.

Rick arrived a few days later, all speedy and bouncy and uncontrollable from his dealings with the world outside. He had been hanging out of helicopters in Borneo this time. He told me that when he went to have the car fixed in Carnarvon the day before, the garage mechanic said, "Hey, have you heard what's happened to your girlfriend? Her camel's sick and she'll be here in mid-November."

Jan and David offered to truck the camels to a spot just half a dozen miles from the ocean. That was fine with me—I was no purist. Besides it was hot.

I was dropped off with the camels. I saddled up and rode those last miles, filled with apprehension. I didn't want this trip to end. I wanted to head back to Alice, or the Canning, or anywhere. I liked doing this. I enjoyed it. I was even reasonably good at it. I had visions of myself spending the rest of my life as a tinker, wandering around the desert with a herd of dromedaries behind me. And I loved my camels. The thought of leaving them was unbearable. And I didn't want Rick waiting for me at the ocean either. I wanted to be alone for that bit. I asked him not to take photos at least. He got that petulant thwarted look. Oh well, I smiled and thought wryly to myself, as it was in the beginning so shall it be in the end. It wasn't all that important. Poetic justice really.

Jan and David wanted to learn all they could from Robyn. "To this day, my friends at Woodleigh are the only people I can really discuss camel behavior with ad nauseam and know that they will understand. They dote on them as much as I do and are virtual slaves to their every whim. Dookie, Bub, Zelly and Goliath had landed on their feet. This was their new home, and they immediately took over." Now that Robyn had settled the camels' future it was time to complete the journey.

*I*COULD SEE THE AFTERNOON SUN GLINTING ON THE INDIAN
Ocean behind the last dune. The camels could smell it and
were jumpy as hell. And here I was at the end of my trip, with
everything just as fuzzy and unreal as the beginning. It was
easier for me to see myself in Rick's lens, riding down to the
beach in that clichéd sunset, just as it was easier for me to
stand with my friends and wave goodbye to the loopy
woman with the camels, the itching smell of the dust around
us, and in our eyes the fear that we had left so much unsaid.
There was an unpronounceable joy and an aching sadness to
it. It had all happened too suddenly. I didn't believe this was
the end at all. There must be some mistake. Someone had
just robbed me of a couple of months in there somewhere.
There was not so much an anticlimactic quality about the
arrival at the ocean, as the overwhelming feeling that I had
somehow misplaced the penultimate scene.

And I rode down that stunningly, gloriously fantastic pleistocene coastline with the fat sun bulging on to a flat
horizon and all I could muster was a sense of it all having
finished too abruptly, so that I couldn't get tabs on the fact
that it was over, that it would probably be years before I'd
see my beloved camels and desert again. And there was no

*It was late afternoon on a perfect
day when Robyn and the camels got
their first glimpse of the Indian
Ocean. The camels had never seen
any body of water bigger than a
puddle before and their eyes bulged
at the infinite expanse in front of
them. They simply couldn't believe
their eyes.*

time to prepare myself for the series of shock-waves. I went numb.

The camels were thunderstruck at the sight of that ocean. They had never seen so much water. Globs of foam raced up the beach and tickled their feet so that they jumped along on all fours—Bub nearly sent me flying. They would stop, turn to stare at it, leap sideways, look at another with their noses all pointed and ridiculous, then stare at it again, then leap forward again. They all huddled together in a jittery confusion of ropes. Goliath went straight in for a swim. He had not yet learnt what caution was.

I spent one delirious week on that beach. As chance had it, I had finished my trip on a stretch of coastline that was unique in all the world. It rimmed the inner arm of an inlet, known as Hamelin Pool. A seagrass sill blocked the entrance to the ocean, so that the water inside this vast, relatively shallow pool was hyper-saline, a happy chance for the stromatolites, primitive life forms that had lived there for 500 million years. These strange primeval rocks rose up out of the water's edge like a bunch of petrified Lon Chaneys. The beach itself was made up of tiny coquina shells, each as perfect and delicate as a baby's fingernail. A hundred yards back from this loose shell was compacted shell, leached with lime until it formed a solid block that went down forty feet or more, which the locals cut up with pit saws to build their homes. This was covered with gnarled stunted trees and succulents, all excellent camel fodder, and behind all that were the

What appeared to be floating rocks in Hamelin Pool turned out to be living coral entities called strom-atolites, one of the oldest forms of life on earth. The only other place they exist is in the Black Sea.

Of all the camels Bub was the one who seemed to be the most delighted by the water even though he couldn't drink it. He treated the water as if it were a newfound toy, splashing around like a toddler. If Robyn was in the water Bub had to be there too.

gypsum flats and red sand swells of the desert. I fished for yellowtail and swam in the clearest turquoise waters I've ever seen; I took the camels (all except Zeleika who stubbornly refused even to paddle) for swims; I crunched my way over the beach that was so white it was blinding and gazed at little green and red glass-like plants, and I relaxed in the firelight under bloodshot skies. The camels were still dazed by the water—still insisted that it was drinkable, even after pulling faces and spitting it out time and time again. Often they would come down to the beach at sunset to stand and stare.

And once again, for the last time, I soared. I had pared my possessions down to almost nothing—a survival kit, that's all. I had a filthy old sarong for hot weather and a jumper and woolly socks for cold weather and I had something to sleep on and something to eat and drink out of and that was all I needed. I felt free and untrammelled and light and I wanted to stay that way. If I could only just hold on to it. I didn't want to get caught up in the madness out there.

Poor fool, I really believed all that crap. I was forgetting that what's true in one place is not necessarily true in another. If you walk down Fifth Avenue smelling of camel shit and talking to yourself you get avoided like the plague. Even your best American buddies will not want to know you. The last poor fragile shreds of my romantic naïvety were about to get shrivelled permanently by New York City, where I would be in four days' time, shell-shocked, intimidated by the canyons of glass and cement, finding my new adventuress's identity kit ill-fitting and uncomfortable, answering inane questions which made me feel like I should be running a pet shop, defending myself against people who said things like, "Well, honey, what's next, skateboards across the Andes?" and dreaming of a different kind of desert.

On my last morning, before dawn, while I was cooking breakfast, Rick stirred in his sleep, sat up on an elbow, fixed me with an accusing stare and said, "How the hell did you get those camels here?"

"What?"

"You killed their parents, didn't you?"

He sneered and gloated knowingly for a second then dropped back into unconsciousness, remembering nothing of it later. There was some kind of rudimentary truth hidden in that dream somewhere.

Jan and David arrived with the truck and I loaded my now plump and cheeky beasties on it and took them back to their retirement home. They had many square miles to roam in, people to love and spoil them, and nothing to do but spend their dotage facing Mecca and contemplating the growth of their humps. I spent hours saying goodbye to them. Tearing myself away from them caused actual physical pain, and I kept going back to sink my forehead into their woolly shoulders and tell them how wonderful and clever and faithful and true they were and how I would miss them. Rick then drove me to Carnarvon, one hundred miles north where I would pick up the plane that would wing me back to Brisbane, then to New York.

In Carnarvon, a town about the size of Alice Springs, I suffered the first wave of culture shock that was to rock me in the months ahead, and from which I think I have never fully recovered. Where was the brave Boadicea of the beaches? "Bring on New York," she had said. "Bring on *Geographic*, I'm invincible." But now, she had slunk away to her shell under the onslaught of all those freakish-looking people, and cars and telegraph poles and questions and champagne and rich food. I was taken to dinner by the local magistrate and his wife who opened a magnum bottle of bubbly. Half way through the meal I collapsed and crawled outside to throw up over an innocent fire truck, with Rick holding my forehead saying, "There there, it will all be all right," and me saying, between gasps, "No, no it's not, it's awful, I want to go back."

As I look back on the trip now, as I try to sort out fact from fiction, try to remember how I felt at that particular time, or during that particular incident, try to relive those memories that have been buried so deep, and distorted so ruthlessly, there is one clear fact that emerges from the quagmire. The trip was easy. It was no more dangerous than crossing the street, or driving to the beach, or eating peanuts. The two important things that I did learn were that you are as powerful and strong as you allow yourself to be, and that the most difficult part

The beach at Hamelin Pool is made up of tiny loose coquina shells. Further back from the shoreline the shells have been compressed over the ages to form a huge solid block. The locals come out with band saws and carve up the beach into building blocks for their homes. Some of the locals artists even carve the blocks to create primitive sculptures.

216

Bub often seemed to respond to Robyn's moods. As the time neared for Robyn to say good-bye, he sensed that things were never going to be the same.

of any endeavour is taking the first step, making the first decision. And I knew even then that I would forget them time and time again and would have to go back and repeat those words that had become meaningless and try to remember. I knew even then that, instead of remembering the truth of it, I would lapse into a useless nostalgia. Camel trips, as I suspected all along, and as I was about to have confirmed, do not begin or end, they merely change form.

Sponsors, Contributors and Friends

Karen Cox Kemp
Tom Kennedy
Trevor Kennedy
Alison Kepper
John Kessler
Brad Kibbel
Leslie Kinloch
Doug & Françoise Kirkland
Robert Kirschenbaum
Kathleen Klech
Kent Kobersteen
Tony Krantz
Judith Krantz
Laurie Kratochvil
Peter Krummel
Kym Krummel
Bill Kuykendall
J. P. & Eliane Laffont
Linda Lamb
Marg & Peter Latz
Stuart Laurence
John Lehman
Martin Levin
Hugh Levin
Abby Levine
David Lewis
Ken Lieberman
John Loengard
Richard LoPinto
Ashley Lovejoy
John Lower
Ian Macintosh
Cheryl MacLachlan
Tom MacPhee
Tony & Judy Maine
Alfred Mandel
Thom Marchionna
John Markoff
John and Annie Marmaras
Susanne Marouka
Brenda Marsh
Lucienne & Richard
  Matthews
CJ Maupin
Mike & Martha Mazzaschi
Stewart McBride
Ian McCarthy
Drew McEachern
Gary McKinnis
Michele McNally
Kerry McPhee
Dilip Mehta
Jim Melcher
Michael Mellin
Kirsty Melville
Amy Merrill
David Miller
Rand & Robyn Miller
Steve Miller
Graham Miller

Barry Minnerly
Pam Miracle
Clement Mok
Terry Moloney
Dianne Mooney
Amy Moore
Marney Morris
Brenda Morris
Graeme Morrison
Ann Moscicki
Sue Moss
Nora Lee Moss
Jacqui Mott
Robin & Boots Moyer
Karen Mullarkey
Mike Murphy
Elizabeth Murphy
Lori Barra Nason
Gracia Neri
Linda Neumann
Richard Neville
Larry Nighswander
Wayne Niskala
Cameron O'Reilly
Justine O'Reilly
Dan O'Shea
Karen Olcott
Jennifer Olmholt
Alan Orso
Gene Ostroff
Mike Ovitz
Bill Pakela
Pete Palermo
Rusty Pallas
Rick Pappas
William Paterson
Daniel Paul
Tyler Peppel
Mike Phillips
John & Janet Pierson
Prue Pike
Kathrine Pledge
Ronald Pledge
Abby Pollak
Elizabeth Pope
Gaye Poulton
Karsten Prager
April Presler
Jennifer Prost
Jeff Pruss
Carole Purkey
Sandy Quade
Michael Rand
Hilary Raskin
Peter Rattray
Barry Rebo
Pamela Reed
Denny Reigle
Spencer & Ann Reiss
Stephanie Rhodes

Ruby Rich
Thomas P. Rielly
Linda Ristow
Barbara Roberts
Ty Roberts
Pamela Robinson
Anita Roddick
Deborah Rodgers
David Rose
Bill & Faye Rosenzweig
Lisa Roth
Roy Rowan
Ben Ryan
Tom Ryder
Mark Rykoff
Paul Saffo
Nola Safro
Lucien Samaha
Bruce Sangster
Debora Sansevero
Carolyn Savarese
Toly Sawenko
Murray & Jenny Sayle
Frank Scales
Phil Scanlan
Fred & Joanne Scherrer
Ellen Schonfeld
Lisa See
Tim Self
Tom Sellars
Kay Sexton
Jonathan Seybold
Neil & Karen Shakery
Kathleen Shehan
Bill Shenker
Robert Shepard
John Shield
John Shingleton
Phil Simon
Robin Simpson
Bruce Sims
Bob Siroka
Richard Skeie
Aviva Slessin

Dick Smith
Megan Smith
Rodney Smith
Stephanie Smith
William Cruz Smith
Rick Smith
Joe Smith
Temple Smith
Leslie Smolan
Marvin & Gloria Smolan
Sandy & Reed Smolan
Mike Solomon
Joy and Marty Solomon
Beverly Spicer
Jim Stein
Bob & Aileen Stein
Murphy Stein
Michele Stephenson
Steve Stepnes
John Stewart
Andy Stewart
Adam Stock
Susan Stocks
Jim Stockton
Dick Stolley
Warren Stone
Lew Stowbunenko
Pam Strayer
Vince Streano
David Strong
Jung Suh
Barbara Henley
Peter Sutch
Benita Swash
Martin Swig
Kathy Tallone
Ron Tanawaki
Michael Tchao
Michael Tette
Paul Theroux
Frank Thomasson
Tom Thompson
Margaret Thompson
Carol & Chris Thomsen

Jim Thylin
John Tilton
Doug Tompkins
Karen Tucker
Geoffrey Tudor
Lois Turel
Neal & Maureen Ulevich
Binky Urban
Eric & Nina Utne
Della Van Heyst
Priit Vesilind
John Ward
Bill & Donna Warner
John & Marva Warnock
Ellen Waters
Ian Watson
Robert Weir
Joshua Weisberg
Adele Weiss
Kevin Weldon
Mark Wexler
Howard Whelan
Peter Whitford
Sherri Wigger
Alana Wilding
Dr. Peter Wilenski
Fred Wilkinson
Dave Willard
Sue Fiske Williams
Marcia & Robin Williams
Thomas Wilson
Dave Winer
Ann Winn
Barbara Wood
Peter Workman
Shannon Worrell
Richard Saul Wurman
Eric Zarakov

Cutting edge technology played a major role in the production of *From Alice to Ocean*. Beginning with Apple's Quadra 700 and 950 computers, Tom Walker and his team designed, produced and previewed the entire book in color, using Supermac's 21" color monitors. This book was also the first ever produced utilizing Eastman Kodak's new PhotoCD technology. Over 600 Kodachrome slides were scanned and digitally stored on PhotoCD's. The color and contrast of each image was adjusted in Adobe's Photoshop 2.0. Using Aldus Pagemaker the images were brought into the layouts and sized to fit the design format. A variety of color printers were used to preview the book including a QMS Model 100, a Rasterops CorrectPrint 300 dye sublimation printer and finally a Canon CLC-500 color [...] driven by an EFI Fiery Controller. The logistics of the book were managed in Symantec's MORE 3.0 and text was edited using Microsoft Word. The editorial team also made extensive use of Apple's Powerbook 170 laptop computers with Global Village's Powerport 9600 Baud Fax Modems. Communication in the office and on the road was made possible by CE Software's Quickmail. Flat and reflective art was input using Apple's Onescan with Light Source's Ofoto software. We gratefully acknowledge the assistance of these companies whose generosity allowed us to be the first to use these new tools for the production of this book.

Book Staff and Advisors

Produced and Photographed by Rick Smolan
Text courtesy of Robyn Davidson from her book, *Tracks*
Art Director: Thomas K Walker, GRAF/x
Editor, Text and Captions: Rita D. Jacobs
Literary Agent: Sonia Land, Sheil Land Associates
Publicity: Patti Richards and David Carriere
Design and Production Assistants:
  Sherri Whitmarsh
  Stephanie Sherman
Editorial Assistants:
  Denise Rocco
  Chris Noble
  Liz Faulkner Rico
Picture Editing:
  Robert Pledge, Contact Press Images
  Jon Schneeberger, National Geographic
  Guy Cooper, Newsweek Magazine
  Barbara Koppelman
Endpage Map Design: Ray Sim, Australia Geographic
Logistics:
  Andy Park
  Ardsley McNeilly
Publishing Counsel: Gabe Perle
General Counsel: Barry Reder
Accounting: Eugene Blumberg
Travel Coordinator: Barbara Henley, Sun Venture Travel
Marketing Consultant: Tracy Nichols
Original editor of Tracks *for Jonathan Cape:* Liz Calder
CD Development staff:
  Creative Director: Ed Boyle, Magnum Design
  Project Manager: Phil Simon, Magnum Design
  Production Manager: Trish Mayers, Magnum Design
  Video and Creative Consultant: Pam Strayer, Magnum Design
  Audio Video Producer: Frank Scales, Magnum Design

Kodak PhotoCD designer: Peter Mackey, Imergy
Audio Rights: Paul Korsten, Braille Talking Book Library
Audio Narration: Beverly Dunn
Reportáge: Doug Menuez
Mockup edit: Amanda Jones, Antiques & Fine Arts Magazine
Special advisors:
  Dave Biehn, Eastman Kodak Company
  Georgia McCabe, Eastman Kodak Company
  Scott Brownstein, Eastman Kodak Company
  Paul McAfee, Eastman Kodak Company
  Claire Donahue, Eastman Kodak Company
  Cliff Deeds, Federal Express
  Ted Wright, Regent Hotels
  Joan Rosenberg, Imageworks
  Satjiv Chahill, Apple Computer
  Paul Wollaston, Apple Computer
  Elizabeth Perle, Addison Wesley Publishers
  Robert Sessions, Penguin Books
  Charles Melcher, Callaway Editions
  Ed & Rena Barnum, Time-Life International
  Phillip Moffitt, Light Source Computer Images
  Jennifer Erwitt, Feline Productions

It took a great leap of faith on the part of many people to publish *From Alice to Ocean.* I am especially grateful to Ray Demoulin, of The Center for Creative Imaging and the Eastman Kodak Company who generously underwrote this book's publication; to John Sculley of Apple Computer whose technology allowed us to create a book of incredible quality in a very short time; to my literary agent Sonia Land, whose friendship, encouragement, and perseverance kept me going; to Phillip Moffitt who provided guidance and publishing acumen; to *National Geographic* magazine for assigning me to photograph Robyn's trip and for allowing me to use my photographs which originally appeared in the magazine; and to my wife Jennifer whose patience, support and insight were so valuable during the production of this book.—*Rick Smolan*